An Urban World
Churches Face the Future

An Urban World

Churches Face the Future

Editors
Larry L. Rose
C. Kirk Hadaway

BROADMAN PRESS
Nashville, Tennessee

4263-39

ISBN: 0-8054-6339-9
Dewey Decimal Classification: 266
Subject Heading: MISSIONS
Library of Congress Catalog Number: 84-12649

Printed in the United States of America

Unless otherwise stated, all Scripture quotations are from the Revised Standard Version of the Bible, copyrighted 1946, 1952, © 1971, 1973.

Scripture quotations marked KJV are from the King James Version of the Bible.

Scripture quotations marked NIV are from the HOLY BIBLE *New International Version,* coypright © 1978, New York Bible Society. Used by permission.

Library of Congress Cataloging in Publication Data
Main entry under title:

An Urban world.

  1. City churches—Addresses, essays, lectures.
2. Evangelistic work—Addresses, essays, lectures.
3. Urbanization—Addresses, essays, lectures.
I. Rose, Larry L.   II. Hadaway, C. Kirk.
BV637.U74 1984   254'.22   84-12649
ISBN 0-8054-6339-9

CENTER
FOR
URBAN
CHURCH
STUDIES

The Center for Urban Church Studies was begun in 1981 as a cooperative effort of the Sunday School Board, Foreign Mission Board, Home Mission Board, Brotherhood Commission, Woman's Missionary Union, and the six seminaries of the Southern Baptist Convention. The Center was created to conduct research and compile information in order to gain greater understanding of how the gospel can most effectively be shared in the urban areas of the world.

This book represents the continuing effort of the Center for Urban Church Studies to inform and challenge the body of Christ, and in particular the part of the body called Southern Baptists, to the reality of urbanization of our world and the need to be better informed and equipped to minister in the urban context. Like our earlier book *The Urban Challenge,* this book is a compilation of chapters from several authors who have different perspectives.

It is our hope this book will inform, inspire, and challenge you toward greater involvement in the great task of reaching the cities of our world with the good news of the gospel.

Contents

Preface

R. Keith Parks

A majority of people on earth will soon live in cities—for the first time in human history. What are the consequences? We cannot see the future, but we know the changes will be vast and we can already see the beginnings of trends that suggest both crisis and opportunity. Our reactions will affect the course of Christian witness into the next century and cannot be taken lightly. This book is part of the effort to prepare for this future which, if nothing else, will be urban.

The changes we see all around us do not imply that all of the past is worthless—the future is built on the past. Nor do the changes we observe determine the ultimate shape of the future. Many things are possible. As we consider new directions for mission, let us cling to the best of what Christians have always held: a compelling set of basic beliefs. At the same time we should be willing to adjust our methods to changing circumstances and not accept the present overwhelming mission challenge as impossible.

Unfortunately, the obstacle to effective Christian witness is often ourselves. For example, some are convinced that a church building, a seminary-trained pastor, and perhaps a missionary on the foreign field constitute a biblical definition of the essential ingredients for a local church. Clearly, however, there is no such prescription in the Bible. Yet this method of church planting is being used in cities all over the world, typically resulting in extreme frustration. As effective mission workers realize, it is impossible to buy enough land and build enough buildings or provide enough missionaries and seminary-trained pastors to make such "ideal" churches available to even a small segment of the world's urban population.

If we fail to adjust our methods, we cut ourselves off from being the witnesses that we are commanded to be. Our failure to change thus produces a change of its own: ineffective efforts to reach a lost world for Christ. However, if we can change we can then continue toward our ultimate goal.

It is easy to look upon the rapid urbanization of the world with despair. Yet this redistribution of the population may actually present the opportunity for our generation to witness more quickly to everyone in the world. Not only does the physical proximity of so many persons allow for more efficient communication of the gospel, but some of the problems inherent in the city can create vehicles for ministry. The concentration of poverty, illiteracy, unemployment, and despair creates a fertile field for planting the gospel seeds of ministry, compassion, and evangelism. For those who are alone the church can provide a family, and for new residents ignorant of city life Christians can offer understanding and the chance for reintegration in a new, redeemed community. There are many ways to minister to the urban dweller, and we must seek them.

Examples and models detailed in this book will be surprising to some readers, for ministry in the city is different—especially in cities where poverty is so much greater and the Christian presence is so much smaller than it is in the United States. It is, however, easy to see the love, the compassion, the concern, and the emphasis on one-on-one witness in these illustrations. The basics are the same here as in true ministry anywhere, but the methodology is different. Each new city and culture has a unique character which calls for a customized approach, and the models are only intended to be suggestive not exhaustive. Careful analysis of each new setting is essential. Through such study, successful techniques developed elsewhere can then be adapted to fit the situation. The result will be a strategy suited to a particular city with its peculiar needs.

My concern is that we as Christians committed to sharing the gospel in the world have not changed quickly enough to cope with the changes that have already impacted the cities. One illustration is in the great dependence on printing presses, books, tracts, and other printed material. With illiteracy so widespread, could passing out thousands of New Testaments be largely a waste of time and money? Perhaps other tools might be more effective. Audiocassettes, radio, videocassettes, films, and television may enable us to preach the gospel before people learn to read. We must likewise examine each of our methods and ask if there is a better way.

This book may seem overwhelming as it presents a true picture of the sheer numbers of people and the magnitude of the problems facing efforts at urban witness. However, I trust that we, as the Christian community, can look at them as opportunities rather than as problems. If we do we will be drawn to the cities and urbanization can be a catalyst for the carrying out of God's eternal purpose. I pray that as we read this book, we will be staggered and overwhelmed by our human limitations. I do not pray, however, for depression. Rather, I pray that once we have recognized our own lack of strength, we will recognize the tremendous power in the gospel message.

To accomplish the great task before us will require commitment on a level rarely expressed: earnest praying by more and more Christians; large sums of money never before available; intelligent gathering and use of all appropriate information; and commitment of lives in careers of mission as well as brief involvement. Reaching the cities must become a high priority.

We must understand that the magnitude of the task is beyond what all Christians together can accomplish. We must open ourselves to the wisdom and power of the Lord Jesus Christ. The same compassion that splashed tears over Jerusalem motivates us as we look at the cities of our day. May we marshal all our spiritual, intellectual, and material resources. May we be instruments in the hand of Jesus to bring the cities of the world into that Eternal City.

1

Urban Explosion: Causes and Consequences

C. Kirk Hadaway   Larry L. Rose

What is happening to the world? Our perceptions come from what we hear, read in newspapers or magazines, and see on television. Unfortunately, what we receive is often mixed. For instance, we might read Robert McNamara's comment that "short of thermonuclear war itself, population growth is the gravest issue the world faces over the decades immediately ahead."[1]

We may also read the story in *Reader's Digest* which proclaimed that population growth is good, and "Since the beginning of recorded time, the standard of living has risen along with population. There is no convincing economic reason why this trend toward a better life cannot continue indefinitely."[2]

Still other input may come from watching one of the many television specials on world hunger. The dying children in Africa do not seem to be experiencing "a better life" despite having the world's fastest rate of population growth. We hear about the rampant, uncontrolled growth of Third World cities where more than 50, 60, or even 70 percent of the population lives in squatter settlements or slums.[3] We hear of bizarre efforts to control population growth such as vasectomies at soccer games in India with the promise of free tickets.

What is happening to the world? Nearly all observers agree that two things are happening: 1. the world is still growing rapidly, and 2. the cities in the developing world are growing even faster.

Persons involved in mission efforts to reach the world for Christ want and need to know what the world is like and how it is changing. For it is only with such a clear understanding that informed plans can be made for future mission strategy. Where is the greatest need? Where will hunger be a problem in the future? Where does urban growth call for additional missionaries? Questions such as this are often asked and too often go unanswered. Yet they are basic to planning our global mission effort.

Within a huge and hurting world the needs are far too great and numerous for Christians in one American denomination or even in many to address. Priorities must be set—based on a clear knowledge of the needs and costs—tempered by the guidance of the Holy Spirit. We can then proceed doing the most good where our efforts are most needed.

To do this we must have knowledge, much more knowledge than we presently have. We need knowledge at a global level in order to get the big picture, we need it at the national level as we compare nations in our planning, and we need knowledge at the local level so that abstract goals and objectives can be translated into plans which affect real people.

This chapter is the overview, a global picture, with insights and examples from continents, nations, cities, and even a few neighborhoods. Efforts are underway to fill out our knowledge with more complete data on nations and the cities of the world, but much more is needed. This is only a beginning, but it is often said, "You have to begin somewhere."

In this overview we deal first with sheer population, because population growth and urban growth are very much related. We will also examine trends and projections for cities of the world.

Current Population Trends

World population currently stands at about 4.8 billion persons and is increasing at a rate of 1.8 percent per year.[4] This is an extremely rapid rate of growth and means that the world is adding about 84 million people, the equivalent of an additional Nigeria, each year. It also means that the population of the world is expected to easily reach 6 billion by the year 2000 and could double to 9.4 billion in less than forty years.[5]

Alarm over world population growth has been sounding for quite a few years now, and despite a decline in the rate of annual increase from 2 percent a year to the current 1.8 percent the "world population bomb still ticks away."[6]

The world was not always in this situation. However, several factors have combined since World War II to produce the current population explosion. The first is the natural tendency of world population to grow exponentially. This means that even though the annual rate of growth may not change, the number of persons added each year tends to steadily increase. At a growth rate of just 1 percent per year world population would double in only seventy years. When populations are small such a doubling may not seem to be a problem, but populations cannot double indefinitely. Why? A famous story gives the answer.

The story tells of a clever courtier who presented a beautiful chess set to his king and in return asked only that the king give one grain of rice for the first square on the chess board, two grains or double the amount for the second square, four (doubling again) for the third, and so forth. The king who did not know about the principle of exponential growth agreed and ordered the rice brought forth. The eighth square required 128 grains, and the twelfth took more than a pound. Long before reaching the sixty-fourth square, the king's coffers were depleted. To fill the final square would require more than 200 billion tons or the equivalent of the total world production of rice for 653 years.[7]

The familiar graph of world population growth shown in Figure 1 illustrates that we are also moving toward "the final square." With 4.7 billion people and our present growth rate we are set to double in less than forty years. In 2024 if we are still growing at the same rate, can the world sustain doubling again to 18.8 billion? Probably not. The present pattern of exponential growth must end—either through efforts to reduce the birth rate or by the more "natural" forces of famine, disease, or war.

The reason this problem did not occur sooner in the world's history is because high rates of death held down the rate of natural increase. For centuries the world grew at less than .07 percent annually.[8] This situation began to change, however, in Europe and North

Figure 1
World Population Growth: 8000 BC to 2000 AD

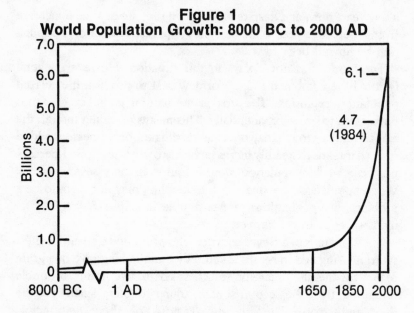

America during the industrial revolution when new farming techniques increased the food supply and decreased the danger of famine and malnutrition. Further advances in disease control in the nineteenth and early twentieth century further reduced the mortality rate and greatly increased life expectancy. Population growth rates increased rapidly as a result of this situation but eventually stabilized late in the nineteenth century and have now reached the point in some developed countries of zero population growth.

The greatest surge in world population growth followed World War II when new health technologies were introduced to the developing world. Rather than the gradual health improvements which Europe experienced, the mortality rate in developing countries "plunged in a matter of decades."9 Cultural expectations for ideal family size did not have time to adjust, nor did the patterns of subsistence which encouraged large families. As a result, population growth in the developing world soared, reaching its highest level in the late 1960s and early 1970s.

At present, 92 percent of the world's growth is occurring in "developing" or Third World countries.[10] Growth is greatest in Africa where the population is increasing at 3.0 percent per year, a rate which will cause it to double in population in only twenty-three years. Latin America is in a similar situation with a growth rate of 2.3 percent per year. The doubling time here is only thirty years.[11]

When we look to individual nations there is even greater disparity in growth rates. Among African nations, Kenya is the "worst" case with a fertility level of 8.0 children per woman. As a result, the nation will double in only 17 years. In Latin America Nicaragua has the highest growth rate, 3.6 percent each year. Unless the rate declines, Nicaragua will double in 19 years. By contrast, in the more developed nations, the growth rate is only 0.6 percent per year and falling.[12] At this pace the developed nations would take 118 years to double in population, and in a few (West Germany, East Germany, Hungary, Denmark, Sweden, and Austria) the population has stabilized or is actually declining.

The rate of natural increase in the world had been increasing steadily into the early 1970s as mortality rates plunged in the developing world. Birth rates were also dropping, especially in industrialized nations, but not enough to slow the rise in an already enormous rate of natural increase. This situation changed in the mid-1970s when the decline in death rates began to level off somewhat in the developing world and birth rates began to drop more rapidly. As a result, the rate of natural increase in less developed countries decreased from a high of 2.4 percent annually during 1965-1970 to an estimated 2.0 percent per year during 1980-1985.[13]

Declines in the birth rate in less developed countries have occurred for a variety of reasons. Rapid growth and its accompanying problems have motivated nations to develop population policies which encourage small families. Whereas only India had such a population policy in the 1950s, now nearly all countries have them.[14] The shift was perhaps greatest in Mexico where the government changed its attitude in the early 1970s from encouraging large families to one which now encourages small families.[15]

Research has shown that the most immediate results in birth rate reduction are produced by making family planning information and services widely available and at no cost to the population. In China such efforts have been supplemented by locally planned birth quotas, financial incentives for small families (penalties for large ones), and by attempts to integrate women into all aspects of society.[16]

Further efforts to reduce the birth rate may be frustrated by the fact that the most significant reductions seem to be tied to social and economic development. In rich countries where children may cost an average of $50,000 each to be fed, clothed, and educated up to the age of eighteen, parents may ask, "How many children can we afford?" But in poor countries, and especially in rural areas, children can actually be a source of income.[17] From the age of five they may be of help with household chores or later with the farm or garden. So here parents may ask, "How many children do we need?" Further, as Elaine Murphy points out, "Couples living in extreme poverty have little reason to think that having fewer children would improve their marginal existence."[18]

Despite the problems associated with further reductions in the birth rate among lesser developed nations, there is some optimism now among those who study population trends that stabilization of the global population may be possible by the end of the twenty-first century.[19] This is, we should add, a somewhat optimistic prediction based on a sustained reduction in the average number of children born per woman from the present 4.6 to around 2.1 (the current level in developed nations is 1.9).

Another reason it may take 116 years or longer for the world to reach population stability is that the world has a great built-in momentum for growth. In less developed countries the largest proportion of society are now children who will soon reach reproductive age. So even if the average family size were to be greatly reduced, the birth rate would still remain high because such a large proportion of the population is of reproductive age.[20] This built-in population growth would then continue until the offspring of the current worldwide baby boom moves past their reproductive years.

As Fox and Haub sum up the situation,

> The fact remains that the Earth entered this century with less than

2 billion population, will close the century with over 6 billion and will probably reach somewhere between 8 and 14 billion when population stabilizes—that is, if the ecological system permits this to occur.[21]

It is a sobering point, but nevertheless a true one, that there are limits to the number of persons that this planet will sustain. If efforts are not made to reduce population growth, shortages of fuel, fertilizer, and food will undoubtedly "aid" humanity in the process.

Recently an article appeared in *Reader's Digest* which pointed out that an average person eats more now than he did in 1960 and that further productivity is held up largely by cultural resistance to modern technology.[22] It follows that the world is seen in no danger of running low on food, and it may even be possible for the world to support as many as 40 billion people.[23] Unfortunately, the true situation is a bit more bleak.

While it is true that per capita production of grain has increased dramatically since 1950, it essentially leveled off in 1971 and has actually declined slightly in the past few years.[24] Because of population growth the world needs 30 million more tons of grain each year, and as might be expected the most serious shortfalls in production are occurring in the developing world. The Soviet Union can afford to make massive purchases of grain to make up the difference when shortfalls occur, but the unintended consequence has been to raise prices and precipitate famines in poorer nations.[25]

Efforts to increase productivity along the lines suggested by Critchfield in *Reader's Digest* depend on the heavy use of fertilizers, pesticides, power for irrigation, and fuel for machinery—all of which, unfortunately, depend heavily on oil and gas.[26] In many developing nations oil and gas must be imported, and increasing the supply to bolster food production will add to already excessive trade deficits. Other problems which have worked against productivity are the loss of topsoil, desertification, salinization, and the defertilization of marginal farmland. Ironically, most of these problems have developed as a result of farmers trying to increase their food production.

Just how many people can the world support at a minimum level of subsistence? Estimates vary according to the definition of such a subsistence level and according to the maximum level of food production that can be sustained by the earth's croplands and seas. Lester R. Brown of the Worldwatch Institute has argued that "supporting even six billion people at acceptable consumption levels would not be possible without sharp increases in food production, widespread food rationing, and more equitable distribution of food resources both within and among societies."[27] Other writers such as Bernard Gilland (1983) use a figure of 7.5 billion as the "maximum carrying capacity" of the earth.[28]

Few experts suggest that the land available for agriculture will increase very much. Indeed, a good case can be made for it decreasing somewhat in the future. Increased food production depends almost solely on increased productivity of existing farmland. If levels in the developing world were to reach those of the United States, Europe, and Japan, the world could possibly support around 9.2 billion persons at the current average level of food consumption.[29] This may well be an unrealistic expectation. More likely, perhaps, is that food production will increase somewhat, but average levels of consumption will decline to even lower levels than today (the average level in the world is only 40 percent of that in the United States and Western Europe).[30]

Despite these problems, the world continues to grow in population and should easily reach the 6 billion mark by the year 2000, a mark that Lester Brown suggests as the maximum world population. Growth is not expected to stop there according to United Nations estimates and is, in fact, not expected to stabilize until it reaches 10 billion in the year 2110.[31] This figure is of course beyond most estimates of the global carrying capacity and will never be reached without serious famines and an overall deterioration in the diets of most people in the world.

World Urbanization

The massive growth of the world's population in recent years has spawned cities larger than have ever existed. In 1950 only two cities, New York and London, were over 10 million. As of 1980, ten cities had reached that size; and if trends continue there will be sixty cities over 5 million, twenty-five cities over 10 million in population, and five cities over 20 million by the end of this century.[32]

Tokyo-Yokohama is the largest city in the world at present with around 21 million people. It will soon be eclipsed, however, by Mexico City, a city that was, until recently, far down the list in terms of size. Mexico City has a population of over 18 million, up from a mere 2.9 million in 1950, and is expected to reach 31 million by the year 2000.[33] The rapid growth of this city and others in the developing world has meant that they are beginning to replace those in industrialized nations as the population leaders. Mexico City will nearly double in population by the end of this century, but other cities in the developing world are growing even faster. The capital cities of Bangladesh and Zambia may triple in size over the next seventeen years, while Lagos, Nigeria, and Nairobi, Kenya may almost quadruple.[34]

The cities of the world are growing at a rate that is twice that of the world's population. As a consequence, the world is rapidly becoming urban. Between 1950 and 1980 the urban population of developing countries more than tripled, increasing from 275 million to just under 1 billion.[35] And at the current rate of growth it could double in only fifteen years.

Many nations which have always had large rural majorities are suddenly becoming urban societies. In 1983 the world had reached 42 percent urban, up from 25 percent in 1950 and 33 percent in 1960.[36] By the year 2000 for the first time in history the world will have a majority of persons living in cities.[37] In this landmark year the urban population of the world will equal the total world's population in 1965.

Historical Trends

The extent of the transition in the world's population can only be understood in the light of world history. Throughout humanity's tenure on earth, the population has always been profoundly rural. Men and women were first hunters and gatherers and later farmers. Villages, towns, and eventually cities emerged for trade, government, and security but the overwhelming majority of the population remained rural. Agriculture was the dominant means of livlihood. This state of affairs persisted for thousands of years. Even as late as 1800 only 2.2 percent of the population of Europe, the most urbanized continent, lived in cities.[38]

The industrial revolution and the advent of the factory changed all of this, at least in Western Europe and the United States. Not only was the economic order changed but also the pattern of residence. It became more efficient for people to cluster together than to be scattered, and cities grew as factories consumed labor. The impact of this revolution was such that by 1900 Great Britain became the first nation in the world to have more than half its population living in cities.[39] Today all of the industrialized nations of the world are heavily urbanized, many with three quarters of their populations living in cities (including the United States).

In general, urbanization in the past century has tended to follow industrialization and economic development. Factories, government agencies, and distribution centers tend to be located in the cities; and if the jobs provided by these major employers did not exist, there would be little reason for rural residents to migrate. Because of this situation, the less developed nations of the world have also tended to be less urbanized.

Since 1950 things have changed drastically. There remains an association between economic development and urbanization, but several other factors have altered the way cities grow in the developing world. First among these is simply rapid population growth in developing nations. Even without migration from rural areas cities in the Third World would be growing rapidly through very high rates of birth. In fact, studies have shown that almost 60 percent of urban growth results from children born to urban dwellers.[40]

Added to the internal growth through births, cities are also growing as people migrate from the rural hinterlands. Without a rapidly developing industrial sector, it is difficult to understand why such large numbers are making the migration to Third World cities. Yet the availability of employment in such cities and the wages paid must be compared to rural areas in the same nations, not to those in fully industrialized states. Migrants generally find their standards of living improved and jobs readily available. They tend to work in what is called the "informal sector" rather than in factories, as street vendors, household servants, ricksha drivers, part-time construction workers, and a host of other often imaginative occupations.[41] In the same way the slums, crowds, and misery present in many cities must be seen in the perspective that conditions in rural areas in developing countries are often worse. According to the *Global 2000 Report,* "food, water, health, and income problems are often most severe in outlying agricultural and grazing areas."[42]

Many countries, such as India and Bangladesh, are experiencing what could be called rural overpopulation. With land use almost totally devoted to agriculture, there is a limit to which farms can be divided and still be efficient. High population growth and an already very large rural population has meant that many persons have had to leave in order to support themselves. There simply is not enough available farmland. For such persons the cities are acting as magnets, offering at least the possibility of a better life. In cities there are jobs, excitement, better educational and health facilities, and the promise of wealth. To those who have lost hope of prospering in the rural environment, and especially to the young who have little to lose in leaving, the pull may be a strong one.

Regional Trends

In the same way that cities in certain regions of the United States are growing much faster than in others, urban growth in the world also varies quite widely. The rate has slowed greatly in the industrialized nations of the world, especially those which are close to 80 percent urban. In the United States, for instance, there was almost no change in the level of urbanization between 1970 and 1980. Increasing urbanization in some areas was largely offset by decentralization in others as technology has made physical location in large cities less essential for some businesses and industries.

Among developing countries a number of trends are apparent, depending on the culture, present level of industrialization, population size, and the degree of economic development. To a certain extent these trends and patterns are regional; for instance, we can talk about Latin American cities in similar terms, and the same is true for cities in sub-Saharan Africa (except for South Africa). In other cases a similar pattern of urbanization can be seen in different parts of the world. There are four clusters in the developing world: (1) Latin American cities; (2) the semi-industrialized nations of North Africa and Asia; (3) sub-Saharan African (except South Africa); and (4) India, Pakistan, Bangladesh, Indonesia, and China. In most Latin American nations the process of urbanization is well underway. Presently, the population in Latin America is 65 percent urban. In most nations incomes are relatively high and there is little pressure on the rural population because of lack of arable land. Urbanization is expected to continue, with most nations becoming nearly 80 percent urban by the end of this century.

Despite relatively high urban incomes for developing nations, the cities of Latin America are characterized by great inequality and the presence of large squatter settlements. Wealth tends to be concentrated in the hands of a small minority while large segments of the population are effectively excluded from the benefits of urban productivity.[43]

The second group of countries is really from two regions, Asia and North Africa, and includes those nations which are semi-industrialized. Such countries have become increasingly industrialized with the growth of manufacturing centers. Urban incomes have risen and along with the scarcity of arable land in some nations have spurred rural-to-urban migration. Overall the urban growth rate in the Philippines, Malaysia, and other "type II" nations is 5 percent annually. This means that the urban sector will be three to four times larger in the year 2000 than it is today.[44]

Africa south of the Sahara constitutes a third region where urbanization has proceeded differently than in the rest of the world. It remains a largely rural continent, despite the fact that many states are presently experiencing massive rural-to-urban migration. This migration has been largely stimulated by urban incomes that are higher than incomes in rural areas. People have been drawn in search of wealth or at least a somewhat better income instead of being "pushed" to the city by a lack of arable land. In most countries agricultural land is not yet scarce and can support larger numbers of people.

The next decade is seen as critical for African cities, setting the basic pattern for future urban growth. Manufacturing and other productive activities are in the incipient stages, and many cities which are expected to be huge are still small enough to be greatly affected by steps taken now. What these cities look like in the future will depend on how realistic the solutions are to current problems.[45] Some may choose the path of Nigeria and essentially "give up" on their largest cities and try to start new metropolitan centers in undeveloped areas. Others, however, may choose more realistic, low-cost solutions.

The level of urbanization in Africa is low, only around 29 percent, but in India, Pakistan, Bangladesh, Indonesia, and China it is even lower (20-25 percent). Despite populations that are largely rural, these nations have extremely large cities and large urban populations. In a sense, they are saturated at all levels. The cities are already overcrowded with inadequate housing and an inadequate supply of jobs. But in the rural areas things are perhaps even worse. There is extreme pressure on the available arable land. No squatter settlements are found here circling the cities. Instead, all available land is tilled, right up to the edge of the city. For this reason greater rural-urban migration is expected in the future with a corresponding massive growth of the cities.

Of all the nations in this fourth category, the situation in China seems the most positive at least with respect to population trends. The extreme degree of control over its people has allowed this nation to greatly reduce its birth rate in only a few years and also to slow migration to the cities. Accordingly, China is becoming increasingly urban but at a pace slow enough to allow the generation of employment and services in its large cities.[46]

Most nations, however, do not have the level of control over their populations that China does. India, for example, has been trying to reduce its level of population growth since the 1950s, and despite certain heavy-handed attempts the growth of its cities and its overall population is still largely out of control.

In sum, there are large differences and many forces at work among developing nations and their cities. Urbanization in Africa is different from urbanization in Latin America, and it in turn is different from China, South Asia, and Northern Africa. We can talk about urbanization in the developing world and contrast it to developed nations, but we should always remember these differences.

Consequences of Urban Growth

People in industrialized nations who are accustomed to the orderly expansion of services and the economic base as their cities grow may wonder how cities in the developing world can become so large. How will it be possible for Mexico City to surpass New York City in size, to reach its projected 31 million in the next sixteen years? Another reasonable question concerns whether or not there is some absolute limit beyond which cities cannot grow—a point where massiveness undermines the economies and efficiencies of urban development and the entire system lies in danger of internal collapse.

George Beier and other experts have concluded that no maximum city size exists as yet because measurement in sheer numbers gives little indication of how large metropolitan areas are structured. The huge cities in the developing world of today and the even larger cities of tomorrow do not conform to the typical American scheme of a central district of high rises surrounded by successive rings of slums, older housing, newer housing, and suburbs. And even in the United States this pattern no longer describes large cities like Los Angeles. Cities grow both by increasing their internal densities through the high-rise development typical of Singapore, Hong Kong, and Caracas, but they also grow through the annexation of new territory. When Mexico City reaches 30 million it will not occupy the same area it does now. It may sprawl over much of the central valley of Mexico and may well have lower population density than today.[47]

Many large cities are essentially accumulations of small cities side by side. The overall urban area grows as these cities merge and also by the creation of new urban cells on the periphery. In much of Latin

America, Africa, and other tropical or semitropical climates the expanding edge of the city is made up of squatter settlements. Despite the lack of even the most basic services such settlements often grow quite large. If not cleared by the government they eventually become permanent.

This sort of uncontrolled urban growth causes problems and as we have seen, results in large part from the uncontrolled growth of population. We cannot, however, say that urbanization in itself is a bad thing for developing nations. It was pointed out in *The World Population Situation in 1979* that "increasing urban concentration of economic activities and population is recognized as a necessary condition, in the long run, for the achievement of economic and social development goals in a majority of developing countries."[48] There are both positive and negative aspects of current world urbanization and our task here is not really to decide whether the good outweighs the bad or vice versa. We only want to understand the situation as it is.

Negative Aspects of World Urbanization. The negative aspects of urbanization in the developing world are probably the best known. We read stories in the newspaper about Calcutta where 600,000 persons sleep on the sidewalks or Jakarta where for the most part sewers, drinking water, and public transportation are not available in a city of 7 million.[49] The stories of poverty, squalor, and decay are found all too frequently. And there is a reason, or rather several reasons. Most basic is the "natural" tendency for air pollution, noise levels, congestion, crime, social disturbances, and health problems to increase along with increases in city size. In fact, these problems appear to increase at a faster rate than does the population.

One of the most serious problems confronting the city in the developing world is that of housing. All over the world the lack of suitable low-cost housing forces city residents to live in slums and squatter settlements. In fact, it has been estimated that over one third of the urban population in developing countries now lives in such conditions, and in some cities the level actually approaches 70 and even 80 percent (see Figure 2). They may be named "bustees" in Calcutta, "bidonvilles" in Dakar, "callampas" in Chile, or "pueblos jovenes" around Lima; but in all cases they are nearly devoid of clean water, sewage systems, trash collection, paved roads, or electricity.[50] Yet even without the most basic of services the urban slums and shantytowns of the world are growing at the enormous annual rate of 15 percent and are expected to double in population in only six years.[51]

Another critical problem which faces many cities in the world is that of pollution. Sewage treatment has not kept up with population growth, leading to the contamination of water supplies with human and industrial wastes. And according to one report this has "set the stage for outbreaks of cholera, typhoid, and hepatitis."[52] Similarly, a haze from the burning of automobile, heating, and industrial fuels, coal, and wood hangs over cities all over the world—increasing the incidence of many respiratory diseases.[53]

The situation in cities of the developing world is oppressive for large numbers of people because of an extremely unequal division of wealth. Most cities lack a middle class of any size. The population is essentially divided into a very small class at the summit which has education, wealth, and power and a very large class at the bottom with next to nothing.[54] This condition is held in place largely by the overall scarcity of wealth, a low level of industrial development, the difficulty in obtaining education, and the severe disparity between rural and urban wages. This latter point is particularly important because it encourages the migration of rural residents who are willing to take almost any job at very low wages. This tends to keep urban wages for unskilled and semiskilled workers very low, both for new and old residents of the city.[55]

As political observers consider the plight of Third World cities and the prospect of massive growth in the future, they are fearful that such conditions will lead to instability. Often the migrants from rural areas feel much better off in the cities, but their numerous offspring do not remember the privations experienced in rural villages. They only see the poverty, the filth, the underemployment, and the huge gap between the rich and the poor. Frustration may be one result, especially when there is little hope for change, and frustration can easily turn into political alienation. With massive numbers in the

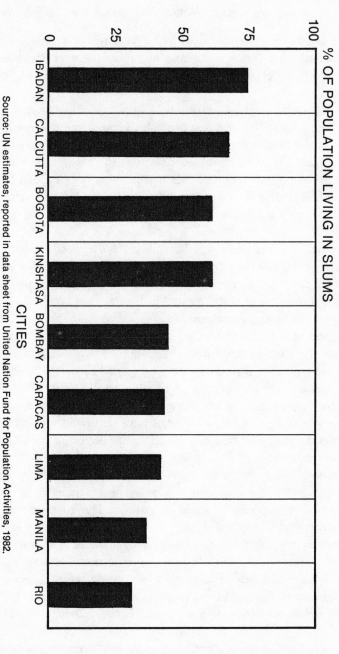

Figure 2
SLUMS AND SQUATTER SETTLEMENTS
CITIES WITH LARGEST % IN SLUMS

% OF POPULATION LIVING IN SLUMS

CITIES

Source: UN estimates, reported in data sheet from United Nation Fund for Population Activities, 1982.

cities vulnerable to exploitation by revolutionaries and other extremist factions, it is no wonder that political observers and the governments in developing countries are worried. They have good reason to be.[56]

Positive aspects of world urbanization. Most would agree that the current rate of world urbanization is much too rapid and that many problems have resulted from the uncontrolled growth. It is easy to point to Lagos, Calcutta, Bangkok, or a host of other cities with festering problems and conclude that urbanization is a problem in and of itself. This view is, however, becoming less and less prevalent among those who study cities and economic development in the Third World.

The root of the problem is not urbanization but the speed at which it is occurring—as it is fueled by massive population growth. Social scientists are discovering that many good things result from urbanization, and some aspects of the trend which were once condemned are now seen as having some real benefits.

One aspect of urbanization which is receiving a new look is the "plight" of the rural-to-urban migrant. Counter to views that such migrants are typically "forced" into the move and end up suffering an even worse fate among the city squalor, studies have shown instead that "most rural-to-urban migrants are glad they moved. They believe that their living conditions have improved, that they are making progress, and that their children are better off."[57] This is not universally true, of course, but overall new urban residents find conditions better in the city than in the rural areas they left.

One major reason for this positive view is that migrants came to the city for jobs and generally found them. Studies have shown that most migrants find jobs quite rapidly, and unemployment rates are often lower among migrants than among urban natives.[58] This may seem hard to believe in light of the fact that in many developing nations the industrial base is so limited. Where do the jobs come from? The answer lies not in what we normally think of as major sources of urban employment but in what is called the "informal sector."

Migrants typically find their first work in street vending, construction, handicrafts, and domestic service. Work is often intermittent, poorly paid and physically demanding, but it is also readily available.[59] The size of the informal sector is quite large, with estimates ranging from 45 percent of all employment in Jakarta, Indonesia, 36 percent in Abidjan and Lagos, and 25 percent in Sao Paulo, Brazil.[60] The informal sector is no longer viewed as a negative phenomenon, but as perhaps the only way that cities in developing nations can avoid massive unemployment and the resulting social unrest.[61]

In some cases the informal sector does an even better and more efficient job at providing certain services than does the formal sector. Native markets are perhaps the classic example. Foodstuffs are available more easily, more cheaply, and often with better quality in the native markets than in any supermarket.[62]

Housing is perhaps the key example of how a problem may be a solution. We have seen that housing shortages are one of the major problems experienced by Third World cities. Shortfalls in construction by the government and the private sector and the lack of low cost housing has led to the urban poor in many cities constructing their own in shantytowns. These were once viewed as harmful, and residents were always fearful of having their homes bulldozed by the government. Recent observations have changed views on shantytowns and they are now seen as "possibly the correct solution for urban development in the Third World—a solution tailored to the exigencies of the poor."[63]

Essentially, it is now seen that there is no way developing countries can afford to build housing, water, electrical, and sewer systems fast enough to keep up with urban growth. The costs are simply too high and would drain funds from projects that are more directly related to the economic development of the nation. Squatter settlements are an example of how the population takes development into its own hands.

Squatter settlements are also not as chaotic as they appear. Recent studies have shown that an informal, but nevertheless strong, social structure develops quite rapidly. The community that forms may in fact "be functioning well and making great efforts to improve conditions."[64] Crime rates are often lower than other areas of the city because of social pressure and the acute awareness by residents of who lives here and who does not. Close-knit networks of interaction exist and facilitate the integration of new residents and provide support in the form of communality, hospitality, and celebration.[65]

In addition, squatter settlements do not remain squatter settlements once the government begins to consider them "new towns" or "young neighborhoods." When land tenure is secure the squatters begin to rebuild their shacks into permanent and substantial dwellings.[66] They also begin the process of trying to obtain the basic services that these areas lack from the government: lighting, water, electricity, garbage removal, roads, and the like. Eventually they become an integral part of the city.

Conclusion

As Christians supporting, encouraging, and engaging in efforts to reach the world for Christ, the cities cry out to us as strategic points where the gospel can be proclaimed to more people with less effort. As Ray Bakke often says, "God is urbanizing His world." This fact, and it is a fact, should cause us to rethink our entire mission orientation. And even if we were to argue that perhaps it is humanity that is urbanizing the world rather than God, the difference really should not matter to us. It is happening. Whether we view cities as exciting good places or decadent evil ones, it is happening: the world is becoming urban.[67]

The urgency of our work in the cities of the world should be apparent in these pages. Because of rapid population growth we have to run hard just to stand still. Growth is largest outside the "Christian world," and as a result our proportion of the world's population is slipping. More people are becoming Christians than ever before, but with such a high birth rate we are not keeping up. In light of this we might ask what our strategy should be. And in terms of effort, there is no doubt that we should strive to reach the cities first in much the same manner as the apostle Paul.

Cities are strategic. People are concentrated there. So are power and wealth. Communication networks flow from cities. Often what happens in a single city so dominates a nation that what occurs elsewhere in the country is almost insignificant. Such is the case in Mexico, Venezuela, Tanzania, Kenya, and a host of other nations controlled by a single primary city. To reach these cities for Christ is to reach their nations but to do this we must first understand them.

Learning a new city is not always difficult if a missionary already understands city life, the culture and language of the people, and asks the right questions. Unlike the apostle Paul, we may not be blest with the prior knowledge and understanding he took into the cities of the ancient world. We can, however, acquire these insights—and we must if we have any hope of being successful.

This chapter is only a starting point in the process of better understanding the world and her cities. We have tried to point out a few features of world population growth and world urbanization which should be considered as mission agencies and Christians all over the world plan and pursue ministry. We have seen, for example, that the world is growing at a rate that cannot be sustained for long. This fact and others we have reviewed suggests a number of possibilities for the future. Famine, social unrest, mass population migrations, chronic housing shortages, and other related problems can be expected to be more frequent and widespread.

What should our response be? Should hunger and medical relief efforts be stepped up? What actions can and should be made to increase crop production without further damage to the land. How should we approach the issue of birth control and family planning. And finally, how can a small mission force expand its efforts so that ever larger masses of persons can hear the gospel proclaimed in their own language? Hard decisions must be made based on accurate information.

We have also seen that the cities are growing much faster than the population in most developing nations. Does this mean that mission efforts should become focused in these urban centers? Can we or should we deal with the problems of the people in the cities: lack of jobs and housing, social dislocation, pollution, noise, lack of water, plumbing, and sanitary facilities. How should we respond to squatter settlements? Should efforts be made to become "part of them"— gaining the confidence of their leaders, supporting them in confrontations with the government? In so doing might we improve their lot and also open doors for the gospel?

In chapters which follow more will be said about such issues by professors, mission agency leaders, and missionaries. Throughout, the big picture is given in order to show the need, and examples are related in order to show what can be done. Efforts are already underway to collect the details on the largest cities in the world so that worldwide priorities can be set and local strategies constructed. Your help may be needed in this process.

Notes

1. Quote from Robert S. McNamara in "The Population Crisis Committee," pamphlet (Washington: Population Crisis Committee, n.d.).
2. Julian L. Simon, "Population Growth is Good," *Readers Digest,* Mar. 1982, p. 118.
3. United Nations, *The Aging in Slums and Uncontrolled Settlements* (New York: United Nations, 1977), publication ST/ESA/55., pp. 10-11. Also, Population Crisis Committee, "World Population and Global Security," (Washington: Population Crisis Committee, 1983), Briefing Paper #15, p. 2.
4. Mary M. Kent, "1983 World Population Data Sheet," (Washington: Population Reference Bureau, 1983).
5. Six billion figure is from Kent, 1983; 9.4 billion figure assumes a constant rate of world population growth.
6. See "The World Population Bomb Still Ticks Away," by Robert Fox and Carl Haub, *Intercom,* Mar./Apr. 1983, p. 10.
7. Population Reference Bureau, "World Population Growth" information sheet (Washington: Population Reference Bureau, 1975).
8. Population Reference Bureau, "World Birth and Death Rates," information sheet (Washington: Population Reference Bureau, 1975).
9. Elaine M. Murphy, *World Population: Toward the Next Century,* (Washington: Population Reference Bureau, 1981), pp. 2-3.
10. Council on Environmental Quality and the Department of State, *The Global 2000 Report to the President,* Vol. 1. (Washington: US Government Printing Office, 1980), p. 9.
11. Kent, 1983.
12. Ibid.
13. Rafael Salas, "State of World Population—1983," *Popline,* July 1983, p. 1.
14. Rafael M. Salas, "Population and the Global Future," Speech Series No. 57 (New York: United Nations Fund for Population Activities, 1980), p. 3.
15. Murphy, p. 6.
16. Ibid., p. 5.

17. Mary Warren, "More Children Than They Want," *Popline,* July 1983, p. 1.
18. Murphy, p. 5.
19. Salas, 1983, p. 1.
20. Office of Technology Assessment, *World Population and Fertility Planning Technologies* (Washington: Congress of the United States, 1982), pp. 36-38.
21. Fox and Haub, p. 10.
22. Richard Critchfield, "Famine Fallacies," *Readers Digest,* Mar. 1982, pp. 119-120.
23. R. Revelle, "The Resources Available for Agriculture," *Scientific American,* Sept. 1976, pp. 164-178.
24. Lester R. Brown, "World Food Resources and Population: The Narrowing Margin," *Population Bulletin,* Sept. 1981, p. 5.
25. Ibid., p. 6.
26. Council on Environmental Quality and The Department of State, p. 2.
27. Brown, pp. 29-30.
28. Bernard Gilland, "Considerations on World Population and Food Supply," *Population and Development Review,* June 1983, p. 206.
29. This figure was computed by the authors using data from papers by Lester R. Brown, 1981, and Bernard Gilland, 1983.
30. Gilland, p. 204. This was measured in terms of gross consumption for all purposes (including waste) divided by the population. If considered in terms of the actual use of food in the diets of persons, the Population Reference Bureau estimates that the average person in developed nations consumes 134 percent of daily calorie requirements while the level for the average person in developing countries is 101 percent.
31. Murphy, p. 1.
32. Ibid.
33. United Nations, *Patterns of Urban and Rural Population Growth,* Population Studies, No. 68 (New York: United Nations, 1980a) p. 129.
34. Population Crisis Committee, p. 2.
35. Population Information Program, "Migration, Population Growth, and Development," *Population Reports,* Sept./Oct. 1983), p. M-247.
36. United Nations, *The World Population Situation in 1979.* (New York: United Nations, 1980b), p. 55.
37. Kent, 1983.
38. Population Reference Bureau, "World Urbanization, 1800 to 2000" information sheet (Washington: Population Reference Bureau, 1975).
39. United Nations, 1980a, p. 7.
40. United Nations, "Urbanization and City Growth," *Populi,* 10 (2, 1983), p. 48.
41. Population Information Program, p. M-257.
42. Council on Environmental Quality and the Department of State, p. 12.
43. George J. Beier, "Can Third World Cities Cope?" *Population Bulletin,* Dec. 1976, p. 5.
44. George Beier, Anthony Churchill, Michael Cohen, and Bertrand Renaud, "The Task Ahead for the Cities of the Developing Countries," *World Development,* May 1976, p. 368.
45. Ibid.

46. Ibid., pp. 368-370.
47. Ibid., p. 376.
48. United Nations, 1980b, p. 53.
49. Benjamin Tonna, *Gospel for the Cities*. (Maryknoll: Orbis Books, 1982) pp. 18-20.
50. Population Crisis Committee, p. 2.
51. United Nations, 1977, p. 10.
52. Lester R. Brown, Patricia L. McGrath, and Bruce Stokes, "Twenty-Two Dimensions of the Population Problem," *World Watch Paper #5*, Mar. 1976, p. 26.
53. Ibid., p. 5.
54. Tonna, pp. 42-43.
55. Population Information Program, p. M-262.
56. Population Crisis Committee, p. 2.
57. Population Information Program, p. M-257.
58. Ibid.
59. Tonna, p. 17.
60. United Nations Conference on Human Settlements, *Global Review of Human Settlements* (Oxford: Pergamon Press, 1976), pp. 42-46.
61. Johannes F. Linn, *Cities in the Developing World* (New York: Oxford University Press, 1983) p. 41.
62. United Nations Conference on Human Settlements, p. 46.
63. Tonna, p. 84.
64. Population Information Program, p. M-263.
65. Tonna, p. 22.
66. Population Information Program, p. M-263.
67. For another picture of the world's population future, see *Planet Earth 1984-2034: A Demographic Vision* by Leon F. Bouvier (Washington: Population Reference Bureau, 1984).

2

Urbanization and Christian Ministry in World History

Winston Crawley

Urbanization is not a new challenge to Christians. The gospel of redemption was born in the city of Jerusalem and exploded into Christian ministry in a chain of cities across the Roman Empire. This urban coloration of Christian ministry has frequently been overlooked in recent generations, and mission efforts have often been focused on smaller towns and villages. The situation has changed, however, because a new burst of surprisingly rapid urbanization has forced all interpreters of the world scene, whether secular or Christian, to focus anew on cities.

Robert T. Handy has reminded us that "systematic study of urban history is relatively new," referring to a pioneering study in the field that was published in the early 1930s.[1] The classic survey *The City in History* by Lewis Mumford was published in 1961. From about that time, an increasing flood of books began to be published focusing on the city from the perspective of Christian ministry. The influential book *The Secular City* by Harvey Cox appeared in 1965.[2]

Some Christian writers in recent decades have felt that Christianity is facing the urban scene for the first time. Of course, it is true that there are many aspects of modern cities that were lacking in earlier eras. But, in principle, Christian ministry has had an urban reference from the beginning.

Urban Ministry in Biblical Times

An often quoted summary statement is that the Bible "begins in a garden and ends in a city." That rather romanticized epigram expresses the pertinent truth that in the historical record of the

Scriptures there is a movement toward greater urbanization. The latter parts of the Bible are set more in an urban context than are the earlier parts. Christianity is a historical religion, and the Scriptures are given to us in a historical setting. The flow toward the cities that is a part of human history is reflected in the Scriptures.[3]

The Old Testament records a progression from the mobile, pastoral family of the patriarchs to the pivotal city of Jerusalem. In the New Testament each of the four Gospels moves from a largely rural and small-town setting in Galilee toward Jerusalem. Jesus' "face was set toward Jerusalem" (Luke 9:53). The tears he shed over the city would be forever sufficient authorization for Christian urban ministry.

When we pass from the Gospels into the Book of Acts and the Epistles, we enter what is largely an urban world. Very little in the record of Acts takes place in a setting other than a city. The Epistles are written—the ones that go to churches—to city churches. At the close of the New Testament, we find the Book of Revelation addressed to churches in what are commonly called "the seven cities of Asia." New Testament Christianity, despite the rural background of Jesus and the rural imagery in his teachings, was predominantly urban.

The urban focus is especially evident in the spread of the gospel as reported by Luke in the Book of Acts. After Jerusalem, the next prominent center of early Christianity was the cosmopolitan city of Antioch. From there the Christian movement progressed steadily on toward Rome, the central city of the Mediterranean world. Along the way, Paul seems to have followed a conscious strategy at the leading of the Holy Spirit, going from one important city to another, seeking to plant churches in the main cities, with the expectation that the gospel would spread from those centers into neighboring smaller cities, towns, and rural areas. Urban evangelization and urban ministry were foremost in that strategy.

If, indeed, the challenge of urban ministry is just being discovered in this century, it is a rediscovery and not something "new under the sun" or new in God's plan for his church. In the long centuries of

Christian history, cities may have slipped out of the central focus of Christian concern, but they have been there since the beginning.[4]

Urbanization and European Christianity

The centrality of the city that was evident in the missionary outreach of Paul and in other parts of the New Testament continued into the early centuries of Christian history. The very terminology of church history reflects it, as these were the centuries in which the system of "metropolitan bishops" was developing. The process is described from a Roman Catholic perspective by Benjamin Tonna.[5] That process resulted in a concept of the parish consisting of all the Christians within a city under the leadership of a bishop.

After Christianity was made the official religion by Constantine, this development was strengthened. "The principle of one parish per city was soon confirmed by legislation: the Council of Chalcedon even made the creation of a new parish conditional upon the unit of a city."[6] Obviously up to this point in Christian history, at least in its administrative arrangements, Christianity was predominantly urban. Any Christians in rural or small-town areas were considered as part of a parish that was centered in the city. According to Tonna, "the first rural churches emerged only in the third century, in northern Italy. In the fourth and fifth centuries they began to multiply in France as well."[7] By that time several major changes were taking place. Christianity was beginning to spread widely through Europe. The bishops of Rome and of Constantinople were already being given special deference. Differences between western and eastern Christianity within the Roman Empire were becoming more evident and more firmly defined. The empire itself was being assailed by invading tribes from northern and eastern Europe.

The city was so central to the life and the thought of Christians that even as Rome was tottering toward its fall, the great theologian Augustine used it as a model for his classic description of Christianity as *The City of God.*

In the medieval period, which began roughly with the fall of Rome, the initial five centuries are often referred to as the Dark Ages. Rome and the other cities of the formerly Roman world were deteriorating. Under continuing barbarian invasions and without imperial power as a protection, population in the cities shrank. In a sense, for several centuries, Europe returned to a life mainly of villages and towns. As the period progressed, the system known as feudalism arose and thrived. Castles and walled towns defended by the armies of local lords gave some security to the peasants and townspeople who submitted to the authority of those lords.

As cities lost the importance they once had, "church structures began to disintegrate under the pressure of the feudal system."[8] In the beginning centuries of the Christian era, the main strength of the church had been in the cities. With the decline of cities in the Dark Ages, the church was having to find ways of adapting to a less urban situation—a problem that was substantially the reverse of the situation faced by the church in recent decades here in the United States and now in much of the world.

The major adaptation made by the church to its new situation was the monastic system. Mumford refers to the monastery as "in fact a new kind of polis" and says that "the closest link between the classic city and the medieval city was that formed . . . by the monastery."[9]

The withdrawal of the major strength of Christianity from the cities into monasteries, with more of an inward focus than an outward ministry, helped the church to survive a chaotic period in the history of Europe, but it also left the church ill prepared for the new urban challenge that would come with the revival of cities in later centuries. By the eleventh century, Europe was moving out of the Dark Ages, and the eleventh to thirteenth centuries became a new period of urban development. In some measure the church had been responsible for that change. During the Dark Ages, Christian missions had reached out to the invading tribes from northern and eastern Europe, and by the eleventh century those tribes had been at least nominally converted to Christianity. Also by that time they had settled into locations that defined the ethnic map of Europe much as it exists today. The result was a new era of relative peace that allowed opportunity for an increased food supply, growth in population, and an expansion of trade—all of which facilitated urban renewal.[10]

During those centuries, feudalism gradually declined. Merchant guilds and craft guilds multiplied in the towns and in the newly developing cities and became the major social organization of the later Middle Ages. By the close of the Middle Ages, universities had also begun to develop all across Europe.

The end of the medieval period and the dawn of the modern age were heralded by the cultural Renaissance which began in Italy during the fourteenth century and reached its height in the fifteenth, spreading on to the rest of Europe in the sixteenth century where it became influential in the beginning of the Protestant Reformation. How did the church respond to the challenge of the new urbanization in the later Middle Ages? Unfortunately, much of the energy of the church was siphoned off by the distraction of the Crusades. From 1096 to 1270, a period of almost two centuries, efforts to regain the Holy Land through seven major Crusades captured the imagination and the resources of European Christendom.

In two major ways the church did have an impact on the life of Europe's cities during those centuries. One was the building of the great cathedrals as central symbols of the place of the church in urban life. Even so, the amount of investment of time, energies, and resources in grand buildings, inspiring and influential as they may be, still must be questioned as to whether it is the best representation of the approach of Jesus and the New Testament to urban ministry.

More obvious "ministry" came from the other major development—the new fraternal orders within the Catholic Church. The earlier orders had been monastic (that is, "living alone"). They had stressed withdrawal from the world for reading, prayer, and meditation. The new orders of friars (that is, "brothers")—Augustinians, Carmelites, Dominicans, and Franciscans which arose in the twelvth and thirteenth centuries were often located in or near cities and engaged in various contacts and ministries within the cities. Christian hospitals and almshouses began to grow from such movements (as did also new missionary outreach beyond Europe).

Tonna points out, however, that in this new urban development both society and the work of the church were fragmented. Urban territory had been divided into smaller parishes, which he interprets as following a rural model. In any event, there was no unified approach to Christian ministries in the cities.[11] Furthermore, the church had adopted a principle of not interfering in public affairs. Harvie Conn traces this principle to the teaching of the prominent Catholic theologian, Thomas Aquinas. He states that the principle "left the world of the city relatively autonomous of the kingdom of God," thereby sowing "the seeds of the secularized city."[12]

Tonna sums up this development as follows: "When the industrial revolution appeared, the church was too distant and too distracted to accommodate itself to it. Just when everything began to happen in the cities, the church had turned to a path that was decisively rural."[13] Tonna implies that there has been little change in the Roman Catholic approach to cities in more recent centuries, and that it is only slowly in our own day that the Roman Catholic Church is reevaluating its approach to urban ministries. Of course, these and other factors in Roman Catholic Europe were setting the stage for the Protestant Reformation. In the early years of the Reformation, Calvin sought to make the church and the city into an almost theocratic system which he undertook to demonstrate at Geneva. Luther developed a theory of two separate kingdoms, spiritual and secular, in an uneasy alliance in which the city belonged to the secular kingdom of natural law and reason. The radical reformers of the Anabaptist movement tended to withdraw from the worldliness of the city.

As it turned out, both in northern (Protestant) Europe and in southern (Catholic) Europe, secularization continued. Increasingly, the church was pushed to the periphery of city life.[14] The trend was hastened by the movement known as the Enlightenment, the French Revolution, and more recently by Marxism and existentialism.

In the meantime, in the wake of the industrial revolution, there was a new great wave of urban development. Francis DuBose describes the resultant industrial city as "metropolis" and notes that it began to have for the first time many of the characteristics we automatically associate with modern cities.[15] The industrial revolution had begun in England about 1770 and had spread rapidly to other nations of Europe (and across the Atlantic to the United States).

Cities grew in size rapidly as laborers came from the farms to the manufacturing centers to become factory workers. Amid the pressures of the city, the new laboring class became largely isolated from the life of the churches.

The evangelical revivals in the eighteenth and early nineteenth centuries brought new spiritual vitality to many in England and in other parts of Europe. The movement included conscious efforts to reach the workers in the great industrial cities. Later in the nineteenth century, the founding of the Salvation Army was another example of concern for Christian ministry to the inner city.

Even apart from open government opposition to Christianity as seen in the Marxist nations of eastern Europe, western Europe has shown a continuing decline for several generations in church attendance and involvement in church life. Large church buildings in most cities of Europe have few worshipers. Many can be maintained only because of government financial provisions for established churches. The free churches have had serious difficulties, resulting sometimes in the combining of parishes and the selling of church properties.

Not only do the masses in most cities of Europe give little attention to the church, but, in addition, the influence of Christianity in all segments of European culture has diminished—so much so that many describe this period in the life of Europe as "post-Christian." At the very least, the cities of Europe are a mission field again.[16]

Even though the term *post-Christian* may imply a false assumption about the extent to which the lands of Europe were formerly Christian, it is more or less appropriate in reference to European culture. Regardless of how little an understanding of Christianity and of genuine personal faith there may have been in an earlier day, there was at least a Christian orientation to culture. Now that has disappeared. The Christianity of most countries of Europe is now rather superficial. In a sense, however, this simply recalls the New Testament situation in which the cities were pagan. Perhaps it is not too much to hope that there can be vital Christian ministry in today's cities as there was in the early generations of the church.

The American Experience

Although this book has primarily a world focus, the American experience with urbanization has great significance for the world mission efforts of American denominations. Our churches have not arisen in a historical vacuum; our outreach to the world is colored by a distinctively American background.[17] Urbanization came later to the United States than to Europe. At the time of the Declaration of Independence, in what was to become the United States, there were probably only five urban centers of 20,000 population or more. Even by 1860, only 16 percent of the nation's population lived in towns or cities with more than 2,500 persons.[18] The main thrust in American urbanization came in the last half of the nineteenth century and the early twentieth century. By 1920, the United States was 51 percent urban, and by 1980 approximately 75 percent were living in metropolitan areas.

The main patterns of church life in the United States had developed before the majority of the people began living in cities. These were developed by rural and small town patterns. Much of the rapid growth in the churches took place during the Great Awakenings in what then were frontier areas. The mainline Protestant groups developed into "overwhelmingly rural denominations."[19]

As the cities developed, much of the population came from new immigration—persons with no history or background of American religious life. Other minority groups, including blacks, came to constitute a large portion of the population of most cities. Furthermore, the mainline denominations, on the whole, failed to reach the industrial workers in the new factories which played such a large part in urbanization.

Southern Baptists have shared in this history. In proportion to population, we have not been strong in the cities. Even where we have large city churches, they often consist of persons who have moved to the city from smaller towns and who perpetuate the atmosphere of country or small-town churches. Thus these churches may not appeal as readily to persons who have grown up in the cities. Some distinctive aspects of the cities (slum areas, industrial labor, high-rise apartments) have been especially difficult challenges to Southern Baptist ministry and that of other predominantly white mainline denominations.

This background poses a problem for American denominations as we expand in Christian ministry to an increasingly urban world. Many or even most of our foreign missionaries have come from rural and small-town backgrounds. In many cases they have had little or no experience in ministry to urban populations. We most likely have remnants of the antiurban bias which has tended to identify rural areas and small towns as Christian in contrast to the wickedness of the city.[20] Ways must be found to surmount the handicap of these background factors if we are to effectively reach an urban world.

Christian Urban Ministry in the Third World

According to United Nations projections, by AD 2000 more than half of the world's population will live in cities. (This projection is based on the varying definitions of urban used by the different nations in their reports to the UN.)

The historical development of urbanization in the Third World has varied greatly from place to place. In very general terms Asia, with its vast population, can be said to have urbanized earlier, followed more recently by Latin America and now also by Africa.[21]

Prior to this century, the industrial revolution had influenced primarily Europe and North America (plus a few other "more developed countries"). Even as recently as 1920, cities in the "less developed countries" had only about one fourth of the world's urban population. By 1980 urban population in the less developed countries had increased almost tenfold, and approximately 54 percent of the urban residents of the world were in less developed countries. "By 2000, Asia is projected to contain 44 per cent of the world's urban peoples, . . . Latin America is to have 15 per cent and Africa 11 per cent."[22]

Popline, the monthly periodical of the Population Institute, reported in July 1983 that:

United Nations projections show that world urban population has been growing at nearly 3 per cent per annum—much faster than the current global population growth rate of 1.7 percent. What is most disturbing about this growth in urbanization is that it will exceed 4 percent per annum in the developing countries. . . . Concern about urbanization arises not from numbers alone, but because a large segment of the urban population will be concentrated in giant cities of the developing countries. In 1950, Shanghai was the only city in the developing countries with a population of more than 5 million. By the year 2000, there will be 45 such cities, mostly in Asia.

Christian missions in the Third World have encountered cities from the very beginning. Early missions beyond the Roman Empire to Armenia and Ethiopia, for example, tended to center in capital cities. This was true also of the famous Nestorian mission in China in the seventh and eighth centuries, and again of the renewed Nestorian missions and the Roman Catholic missions to the Mongol Dynasty in China in the thirteenth and fourteenth centuries. Thus those earlier missionary endeavors seem to have been largely urban.

When we come to the modern period of missions, efforts spread rather quickly beyond the major cities. One example is the ministry of J. Hudson Taylor who intentionally went beyond the main coastal cities to the towns and villages of interior China.

There are now clear differences between countries, both in the degree of urbanization and in the relative responsiveness of rural and urban people. A few countries are highly urbanized with many large cities. A fairly large number of countries have one main metropolitan center. Other nations still today are predominantly rural.

In some countries such as Japan, the response to the gospel has been almost entirely urban, with rural and village ministry encountering much more resistance. In many other countries, the villages today are ripe harvest fields whereas persons in the cities are much less open. These differences become factors in strategic planning for Christian ministry and in the location of missionaries according to their gifts for different types of ministry.

One interesting development that seems to operate as a hindrance to urban missions is the common stereotype of missions in terms of rugged pioneer situations. Many persons automatically visualize the foreign missionary far out in "the bush" preaching or ministering to half-clothed savages. The more likely reality of the missionary caught in a traffic jam in a major city may not be considered "real missions" to some. Ironically, both volunteers and financial backing often seem easier to secure for the romantic frontier.

In many lands, urban populations have been relatively neglected. For example, when Southern Baptists conducted a survey prior to entering Vietnam, it was discovered that more than half the missionaries serving in that country were working among the tribal groups in the hills rather than with the more numerous lowland Vietnamese people in the cities and large towns. There are still many mission organizations that focus on relatively remote tribal groups—which is part of the reason that Southern Baptists have sought to give considerable emphasis to the majority of unreached populations in the major towns and growing cities of the Third World.

By now, of course, there are strong indigenous Christian groups in most countries. They have their own missionary efforts within these countries, and increasingly they are developing mission agencies for international work. Some of the most encouraging and most stimulating approaches in urban Christian ministry today are those that are being developed by Third World Christians (of which examples will be given elsewhere in this book).

The Urban Challenge Today and Tomorrow

By now planners for Christian world missions are aware of the worldwide urban challenge, are analyzing the situation, and seeking ways to meet the challenge. This awareness has developed only in recent decades. This is evident from the writings of Kenneth Scott Latourette whose analysis of world conditions and Christian world missions have been unequaled. The word *urbanization* does not appear in the index of his book *Missions Tomorrow* published in 1936. The central chapter describes fourteen "forces and movements which are making the new day" in Christian world missions. Urbanization is not listed. There is only incidental, passing reference to the cities and urban life. Twelve years later, in another book *The Christian Outlook* Latourette did list urbanization in the index but devoted only one page to the challenge of urbanization in his chapter on "The Current Threat and Challenge."

In the past thirty-five years, both the mushrooming of cities and the awareness and concern of mission planners have come a long way. In 1982 the foreign missions study for Southern Baptist churches focused on urban ministry using Bangkok as a model.[23] The October-November 1982 issue of *The Commission,* the Foreign Mission Board's (Southern Baptist Convention) periodical, expanded on the same theme.

In our new awareness of an urbanizing world, we have often felt stunned by the rapid growth of megacities, especially in the Third World. No city was as large as a million persons before 1800. By 1900 there were eleven cities with more than a million inhabitants; with the exceptions of Tokyo and Calcutta, all were in Europe or the United States. By 1980 there were 235 cities with more than a million people. The number is projected to reach 439 by the year 2000 with 25 cities of more than eleven million persons each. Twenty-two of those twenty-five cities will be in the Third World.[24] The most recent United Nations studies have indicated some decline in the rate of urban growth, but the prospects are still staggering.

When we try to project urban ministries in so many megacities, we feel ourselves paralyzed by limited resources. The number of workers available—especially those with a calling and training specifically for urban ministry—is very small. Financial resources are sufficient for only a minimal approach if traditional patterns of ministry are followed.

Furthermore, work in major urban centers is difficult. The many complications of urban ministry often produce frustration. The social and economic problems of city people are immense. Secularism and pluralism become barriers to the gospel. Views held commonly by Christian people toward the city are a further hindrance.

It is just these imposing obstacles that make urban ministry such a tremendous challenge for Christian missions in the future. Ways must be found to make an appropriate Christian impact on the central city, on the neighborhood undergoing change, on the slum area, on the suburban sprawl, and indeed, on the entire city. Models must be found that can be effective and transferable without dependence on continuing transfusions of resources from outside.

In response to this challenge, the Southern Baptist Foreign Mission Board has entered into a special research project with David B. Barrett, editor of the *World Christian Encyclopedia,* and with the Center for Urban Church Studies. The goal of the project is to analyze the current religious situation and the prospects for Christian urban ministry in the roughly 2,200 cities of the world that will have populations of 100,000 or more by AD 2000. Such analyses are an important part of planning for more intensive and effective urban ministry.

Most urgently needed will be the investment of individuals who are willing to live and minister in these cities. One of the major needs in foreign missions today is a growing number of new missionaries who are specialized in urban work or willing to become so. This will involve a departure from our predominantly rural or small-town viewpoints and practices of the past. The God who cared so deeply for Nineveh and for Jerusalem surely wants his people to share more deeply his concern for the great world cities of our day.

Notes

1. Robert T. Handy, "The City and the Church: Historical Interlockings," in Kendig Brubaker Cully and F. Nile Harper, (eds.), *Will the Church Lose the City* (New York: World Publishing Company, 1969), p. 89.
2. Helpful bibliographies can be found in Cully and Harper, 1969, and in Francis M. DuBose, *How Churches Grow in an Urban World* (Nashville: Broadman Press, 1978).
3. I will not pursue here a detailed treatment of the importance of cities in the Bible and the relevance of biblical symbolism and biblical models for urban ministry today. I have dealt with these concerns extensively in Bible studies presented at a conference on urban evangelism, Manila, Philippines, 1978, and published in the report of that conference.
4. For a description of how churches grew in urban centers in the first century see DuBose, chapter 3.
5. Benjamin Tonna, *A Gospel for the Cities* (Maryknoll: Orbis Books, 1978), pp. 123-125.
6. Tonna, p. 125.
7. Ibid.

8. Ibid., p. 126.
9. Lewis Mumford, *The City in History* (New York: Harcourt Brace Jovanovich, 1961), pp. 246-247. Mumford describes these churches during the medieval period in detail in chapter 9, "Cloister and Community."
10. Mumford, pp. 253-256.
11. Tonna, pp. 126-127.
12. Harvie M. Conn, "The Kingdom of God and the City of Man" in Roger S. Greenway, ed., *Discipling the City* (Grand Rapids: Baker Book House, 1979), p. 17.
13. Tonna, p. 127.
14. The process is interpreted philosophically by Conn, 1979, pp. 21-28.
15. DuBose, pp. 22-23.
16. John David Hughey, *Europe a Mission Field?* (Nashville: Convention Press, 1972).
17. For further detail, see Larry L. Rose and C. Kirk Hadaway, eds., *The Urban Challenge*, (Nashville: Broadman Press, 1982), pp. 11-15 and *passim*.
18. Cully and Harper, pp. 78, 92.
19. Rose and Hadaway, p. 12.
20. Josiah Strong in 1885 listed the city as one of seven perils confronting the United States and as almost a summation of all the others perils. (See Handy, p. 93.)
21. There is an interesting sociological analysis of Third World cities in Tonna, pp. 40-46.
22. These figures and much additional statistical data can be found in the report of an International Conference on Population and the Urban Future held in Rome in 1980. The document was produced by the United Nations Fund for Population Activities. The quotation is from page 15.
23. See Ronald C. Hill, *Bangkok: An Urban Arena* (Nashville: Convention Press, 1982).
24. See Mumford, p. 529, and the report of the International Conference on Population and the Urban Future, pp. 24-28 and Table 9.

3

Urban Poverty
as a World Challenge

Francis M. DuBose

Urban poverty is one of the most awesome realities facing the modern world. Its impact on society is profound, and it offers the church today one of its greatest challenges. Some 45 percent of the population of the world reside in and near cities; and because most of this population is Third World, the majority of these people are poor.[1] From the shantytowns of Africa, Latin America, and Asia to the slums and ghettos of Europe and North America, the urban poor eke out an existence in varying degrees of deprivation.

The Impact of Urban Poverty Worldwide

In the North Atlantic world (Western Europe and North America), the urban poor live usually within the inner city or the "city centre." In the Third World the urban poor usually cluster in pockets of poverty around the rim of the city. Whatever the locale, we see essentially the same kinds of deprivation: social, cultural, economic, political, psychological.

Europe

Urban poverty is found in varying degrees on all the continents. Even Europe, with its long history of industrial prosperity and cultural richness, has always had its urban poor. Modern advantages and reform have not eliminated the chronically unemployed and underemployed, the socially marginal people caught in a vicious cycle of social stultification, political powerlessness, and psychological despair.

European cities have now added to the burden of their traditional poor the new yoke of persons from former colonies who came for jobs that have now ended or which never materialized. In some cases these people were recruited in the prosperous years just after World War II from the poverty-stricken areas of the Mediterranean and sub-Saharan Africa and from Asia and the West Indies. They constituted a cheap working force in the homeland of their former colonial masters. Literally millions of these people now live in the European cities alongside the traditional lower working classes. In France there are millions from North Africa, in England multitudes from Africa, Asia, and the Caribbean. The usual problems of drug trafficking, prostitution, delinquency, vagrancy, alcoholism, and other vices have developed in the wake of this urban poverty.[2]

North America

In North America the problem is similar to that of Europe but compounded by the unique social history of the United States and the legacy of institutional slavery. It is now estimated that the usual 15 percent poor (hard-core and marginal) has increased, and that some forty to forty-five million Americans are at or below the poverty level. For generations older cities such as New York have had their slums and ghettos, which have been the scene of an intergenerational culture of poverty. Add to this the millions of white and black unskilled persons who have been driven from the tenant farms to the cities by the agrarian revolution of the last few decades. The elderly among these poor are particularly victimized by this process. Blacks, Native Americans, Hispanic, and Asian ethnics share in the impact of this social deprivation.[3]

The problem has been compounded by recent internal and external changes. Internally, the jobless crisis has placed families, women, and children in the soup lines traditionally frequented mostly by males. The growing street people culture emerging out of the sixties has swelled the already extensive ranks of the traditional homeless and the urban vagrants. Changes in sexual mores have added a new generation of single parents in the inner cities. Externally, the situation has been complicated by a flood tide of refugees from Asia (Vietnam, Laos, Cambodia) and the Caribbean (Cuba and Haiti).

Added to the usual flow of undocumented persons from Mexico are the refugees from recent political crises in Central America.

With the loss of thousands of jobs by the formerly steadily employed working class because of economic recession and a capital intensive technology and economy, the new immigrants and refugees compound the jobless situation to the point of major crisis. Already a new "yellow peril" mentality is emerging to add to the atmosphere of discrimination which is still deeply felt by many blacks, Hispanics, and native Americans. This fierce competition in a limited, unskilled job market, the virtual collapse of low income housing, and tragic cutbacks in welfare benefits and services have bought urban poverty in the United States to a critical level.

Australia

Even smaller developed nations, which we usually do not associate with the problems of poverty, do not escape this world phenomenon. Australia, for example, has a poverty problem that rivals if not exceeds that of the United States, involving some two million of the country's fourteen million. The traditional poor—the elderly on inadequate fixed incomes, the unemployed, the migrant, and broken families—are now joined by multiplied thousands of immigrants from eastern and southern Europe and refugees from Asia. This picture is tragically compounded by Australia's oldest social problem, the discrimination against the continent's dispossessed aborigines. These groups constitute a vast company of voiceless and powerless persons existing in varying degrees of urban poverty.[4]

Latin America

In Latin America, the push-pull process—the "push" of rural poverty and the "pull" of urban promise—has been hurling people at a rapid rate into the urban centers since the beginning of the Great Depression in 1930. The majority of the Latin American population now live in or near the urban centers of the various nations. Most urban dwellers are these urban poor. They live in the mushroom cities (*callampas*) that have sprung up almost overnight adjacent to and in many cases surrounding the traditional cities. Those who do

not live in shacks and "lean-tos" often crowd together several families in one apartment and sometimes in one room. In some of the
low income apartment complexes, life is so poorly motivated that the
debris in the corridors may be ankle-deep and in some cases almost
knee-high.

The urban sprawl has come so recently and rapidly that it has been
impossible for the cities to provide the common amenities taken for
granted in the traditional cities, especially of the Northern Hemisphere. Entire families migrate to the cities expecting to find jobs and
a better life. They crowd up with relatives and create near, if not
completely, intolerable situations. When work is available it is usually menial, and the income is inadequate to provide the wherewithal
for sufficient urban living. Incomes are often supplemented by beg-
ging and prostitution. Theft in some cities has reached epidemic
proportions. Thousands of orphans and abandoned children roam
the city streets of Brazil. The "hope" of the "urban pull" often turns
to despair, and the result is usually the dehumanizing mentality of
resignation, especially among the middle-aged and elderly. However, an inherent optimism, often characteristic of youth on the
other hand, turns hope to anger and creates the climate for revolution.[5]

Africa

In Africa the push-pull syndrome operates much as it does in Latin
America, often with strikingly similar results. However, it is usually
the African male who first tries out the city before bringing his family
from the village. Although the women and children may be spared
the trauma of the change, the family still suffers. Often the men
never return, leaving the women and children to fend for themselves
in the villages. Sometimes men take on new wives and the added
burden of new families.

Even when the mother and children join the father the extended
family of the village culture is often broken up, and the elderly are
sometimes left without the traditional support of the younger and
more productive members of the larger family support system. Partial or full detribalization often makes for a deep identity crisis and

a loss of a sense of community and belonging. The result can be devastating in terms of social and cultural alienation.

The usual rural-urban migration within certain countries is often intensified by refugees from neighboring nations fleeing the abuse of oppressive political regimes or the despair of critical economic systems. This creates a social climate conducive to riots and general instability. A high illiteracy rate leaves most of the African urban poor—even the youth—with little hope for the future.[6]

Asia

The burgeoning cities of Asia house the heaviest concentrations of people on the face of the globe. Fleeing rural poverty and sometimes moving in caravanlike procession into the cities almost as if by prophecy, they have created enormous problems for the developing nations of Asia. And the urban poor themselves become the ones who are most victimized by the process. The cities of Asia have the highest concentration of malnutrition, illiteracy, and related ills in the world—by the sheer reality of population. The slums of the old city Cairo, the poor of war-torn Beirut, the shifting slum towns of Turkey—all illustrate the reality of urban poverty in the Middle East despite the vast riches of the region's oil economies. The urban masses of the cities of Southeast Asia have one of the lowest standards of living in the world.[7]

The urban poverty of India, Pakistan, and Bangladesh is the most extensive in range and intensity to be found anywhere in the world. When we realize that the population of India exceeds that of the entire Western Hemisphere and that the great majority are illiterate and malnourished, we can only begin to imagine the depth of the poverty in these mushrooming cities. One has to see the poverty of Calcutta to believe it. Over three fourths of the population live in the overcrowded tenement and bustee (slum) quarters of the city. Over 57 percent of the families (extended families) live in one room, and an estimated one million live on the streets completely unsheltered.[8]

The poverty of India is compounded by the nation's centuries-old caste system, which, though officially outlawed, is a *de facto* reality in the nation. The untouchables have poured into the cities in recent years partly to find protection in numbers from the devastating discrimination, if not life-threatening existence, in the villages. A knowledgeable Indian author and champion of the untouchables has said:

> They are not only paupers but centuries of protein deficiency has made them dullards, physically weak, mentally retarded, socially out-castes, economically impoverished. They lead the life of animals.[9]

The Acute Problem of Urban Poverty in the Third World

Although urban poverty is a worldwide phenomenon, there is a marked difference in the extent and degree of poverty between the industrialized world and the developing nations. There is perhaps more widespread poverty in the developed nations than most realize or are willing to admit. However, it hardly compares with the poverty of the less-developed nations. Between one fifth and one fourth of the world is in absolute poverty. Most of this is in the Third World, and an alarmingly increasing amount of this is in the rapidly expanding Third World city.[10]

This difference in economic development is rooted in the fundamental difference between the histories of urbanization in the cities of the Northern tier (Western Europe and North America) and the cities of the Southern tier (southern and Southeast Asia, Africa, Latin America). The cities of the Third World have developed in history more from a political than economic process. They developed from the ruler's decision, not from a revolutionary economic process, as in the case of the industrialized cities of the North Atlantic world.[11]

In the great colonial expansion of the North Atlantic nations in the Third World, an industrialized technology was imposed on the traditional cities. In this system which was designed for the economic benefit of the colonial nations, the basic social structure of the traditional society was not fundamentally changed. The ruling class and the majority poor remain separated in the traditional pattern of their two class system; and though the new urban elite now share in the new wealth brought by the colonial masters which continues through the neocolonialism of today, the great majority of the people remain poor. They continue their traditional survival role without being an essential part of this economic process. This is true despite the fact that some may be a part of the work force which makes this wealth possible. Little or no middle class has emerged through the industrial growth of the colonial and neocolonial Third World city. This is in stark contrast to the development of a strong middle class though the historic Industrial Revolution of the North Atlantic world.

The development of Third World cities has not emerged through an indigenous economic process. It has not come from factors inherent in the culture and society. There has been no Industrial Revolution, and therefore the urbanization has not produced a relatively affluent, literate, middle-class majority as was the case of the Industrial Revolution of the North Atlantic World.[12]

Third World Governments: Nondevelopmental in Purpose

The typical pattern in developing nations is for governments to become joint owners with the multinational corporations. Consequently, both share in the industrial profits. Of course, in this arrangement a vast amount of the industrial profit goes out of the country. This is a system not fundamentally unlike the colonial process—thus the designation neocolonialism. This arrangement as a principle is understandable and in light of the given situation is perhaps unavoidable. The problem is the potential for abuse inherent in this system.

In terms of any substantive benefit to the economic development of the country, the problem is compounded by the way in which the industrial profits which remain in the country are ordinarily used. They are used to run the newly developed government. The strain to provide the most essential functions of government is a great burden on these inexperienced political establishments. Often funds are expended to enhance the image of the new nation through expensive buildings and related projects. When this less than ideal operation is plagued with problems of waste and corruption (which is common), the problems are compounded. It is not surprising how little of the industrial profits go toward the economic development of the country. The added problems of local wars and internal political conflict further drain these limited resources. The result can only be an highly impoverished situation.[13]

Tragic Social Consequences of Nondevelopment

Because its industrialization is nonindigenous and because of its dependence on outside capital, the Third World city is caught in a web of neocolonial interdependence. This is in clear contrast to the city of the developed nations which has always maintained a close working relationship with its surrounding region. Conversely, the Third World city operates, so far as economics are concerned, largely unaffected by its surrounding region.

The consequence of this nondevelopmental industrial "development" is that the usual benefits inherent in classical urban-industrial development have not come to the Third World city. The lack of significant economic development is reflected in a very fundamental means of measurement—education. The illiteracy rate in the cities of the Third World is not appreciably different from that of the rural areas and is woefully below that in the developed nations.

Another striking phenomenon is the birth rate. In the Third World city there has been little decline in extremely high rates of birth. This is in strong contrast to the marked decrease in the birth rate which came in the wake of the industrial revolution in the West. Unskilled, illiterate adults with large families find life in the city extremely difficult. The whole complex political, economic, and social realities of the Third World city make for a level of poverty which is staggering in its challenge.[14]

The Persisting Problem of Slums

Although much poverty can be found in the larger transitional areas of the cities especially in the developed nations, the greatest concentration of poverty the world over is found in the slums. From the barrios of Latin America, the bustees of India, and the ghettos of the United States, there is a common condition which makes the reality of the slum one of the most persistent problems in urban life around the world. The slum is the major social context for physical, emotional, and moral deterioration in the city. It is where urban poverty is seen in its most obvious reality and its most dramatic dimensions.

Characteristics of Slums

Slums are characterized by inadequate housing, if we are justified in calling some slum dwellings housing at all. In Turkey, the word *secekindu* is used to describe a whole community of makeshift homes which are built after dusk and before dawn. In Chile these overnight urban dwellings are called *callampas* (mushroom cities). In the more "permanent" dwellings of slum areas, the housing is substandard by almost every means of measurement. These features are: inadequate street design ("nondesign"), unsafe construction, overcrowding of buildings on the land, excessive density of residences (too many people for the space available), unsuitability for residential use, obsolete buildings (not suitable for improvement), health hazards because of the lack of facilities, and safety hazards because of deterioration. A slum may have one or more of these demoralizing features, and some have all of them.[15]

A slum is a residential area. It may be near an industrial area. Indeed, it may be a place converted from a former or partially functioning industrial area. However, it is a place where people live. It may be large or small. It may be temporary or permanent. But it is a place where men, women, and children have to live in conditions fundamentally unsuited for the most basic expressions of any reasonably meaningful way of life. It is therefore inherently dehumanizing and demoralizing. It is both the cause and result of poverty, and it is the place where the vicious cycle of poverty is lived out to its most inhuman expression!

Related to the problem of substandard housing is the problem of overcrowding and congestion. Cities are characterized by density, but density in and of itself is not a negative social reality. However, when the residential density of any given area becomes unrealistic and compounded by other problems, it is no longer density but congestion. Such is the situation with much of the overcrowding which is characteristic of some slum areas. It has been estimated that if the density in the general population of New York City were as high as the density of certain blocks in Harlem, the total population of the United States would fit into the five buroughs of New York City. In the slum areas of Bombay, India, some 400,000 people reside within a square mile. It is common in Third World cities for as many as ten people to share one room.[16]

This problem of congestion is compounded by inadequate facilities. In slum areas, poor community services parallel poor and congested housing. Such basic amenities as schools, health services, and recreational facilities are usually lacking. Such basic services as water, electricity, and sanitary facilities are very limited, if not nonexistent, in the slums of the Third World.

Inadequate facilities in slums result in a serious lack of sanitation and the consequent threat to health which is typical of life in these depressed areas. In many Third World cities the majority of the people are infested with intestinal parasites. In the United States, the slums yield an unusually high percentage of a city's health problems. The slums of New York City and Detroit, for example, have an infant mortality rate which is twice as high as that of the city at large. Studies have revealed the startling fact that the slum area of an American city, which at its highest could be no more than 20 percent of the population, will have some 50 percent of the city's diseases.[17]

Related to this physical decay is the moral decay in the slums. The slums are characterized by the morally eroding effect of deviant behavior. They have the highest concentration of social problems in the city: crime, juvenile delinquency, drug abuse, alcoholism, prostitution, illegitimate births, mental breakdowns, suicide, divorce, and other personal, domestic, and community problems. As a rule, slum dwellers generally subscribe to unconventional moral codes. Even though there has been a marked departure from traditional moral values among the middle classes, there is still a much more pronounced departure among slum dwellers. However, there are many poor persons in or near slums—the elderly, the mentally retarded, the physically handicapped, families newly unemployed, and others

—who do not contribute to this destructive aspect of the slums but are usually victims of it.

Slum life is strongly isolated from the conventional life of the city. The poor are depersonalized, alienated, and victimized by almost every aspect of life. This leads classically to social apathy. The slums build a psychology of despair. Victims of the culture of poverty in slums and ghettos become indifferent not only to society but often to themselves. However, it should be emphasized that even in the slums, social isolation from the mainstream of urban life often leads slum dwellers to come closer together and to achieve some degree of community as a subculture of the larger urban life. We shall emphasize this aspect later.

Types of Slums

Slums have always been a pronounced dimension of urban life. However, today the vast extent of urbanization has created a complex variety of slum domiciles. One of the oldest and most common forms of the slum is the congested and dilapidated tenement complex. This type of slum is more common in Europe and North America, but it can also be seen in such Asian cities as Hong Kong. In fact the tenements in Hong Kong are some of the most congested in the world. In the cities of India, this type of slum is also common.[18]

In the recent decades characterized by rapid urbanization, another form of slum dwelling has come into prominence. It is the squatter village shantytown. This phenomenon is common in Asia, Africa, and Latin America and is usually found around the rim of the cities. In some places whole shanty cities have emerged near planned cities as in the case of Tema, Ghana, a major port city near the capital of Accra. Often these squatter towns emerge overnight (in some cases literally). The mushroom cities (*callampas*) of Chile and the *secekindu* (built after dusk but before dawn) of Turkey are classic examples of these "overnight" or "mushroom" towns.

The building materials consist of a variety of makeshift items: tin, cardboard, bamboo, scrap wood, straw, and mud.[19] The squatters usually utilize such areas as unused government land, speculator real estate, and undesirable areas which have not been previously used for building construction for obvious reasons. Examples of this type of land which has been occupied by squatter villages are the floodlands of Baghdad, the swamp areas of Bangkok, and the steep hillsides of Rio de Janeiro.[20]

These communities usually have no amenities, often not a solitary water spigot, and certainly no electricity. Because they are squatters, the cities provide no services to them; to do so would be to acknowledge that they exist. It is not uncommon for them to disappear as quickly as they emerge—especially if they become an embarassment to the government or the city elite. They only reappear somewhere else, for the simple reason that the crucial need for housing has not been met. The people have to survive one way or another, and this is one way they do so.

Another type of urban slum that exists somewhere between the congested tenement complex and the shantytowns is the residential slum. These slum dwellings differ from the large tenement complexes in that they are not as crowded and, therefore, are not as congested. The dwellings are most often single story buildings and not massive multistory flats, though it is common for several families or extended families to occupy a single unit. The community will have a water spigot for every so many dwellers, usually very inadequate, causing people to have to walk long distances for their water. Electricity is not a common feature. Toilet facilities are usually outside and are tragically inadequate. In some cases, incredibly, no latrines are provided. People simply use certain designated open areas, beaches, or riversides. This phenomenon is not uncommon in the Third World.[21]

The major difference of these slums from the squatter communities is that they are recognized residences; therefore, token amenities are provided though they are painfully inadequate. Unlike the squatter shanties, they are permanent (as permanent as they can possibly be). As a rule the dwellings are superior to the squatter shacks but often barely so. In many African cities, these types of communities may comprise most of the residential area. The bustees of India are classic examples of these types of slums. Unlike the squatter communities, these residential slums may be found in the central cities as well as the outskirts, especially in Africa, India, and other Asian cities. Although this type of slum is more common in the Third World city, it also exists in the cities of the North Atlantic. One may be startled to observe such a phenomenon as a squatterlike residential unit extending out from an ancient viaduct in the city of Rome.

Another type of slum may be called the "slum town." It may be relatively new-built as a part of an "urban renewal" program. However, its social makeup is such that it does not take long to degenerate into a slum. Such areas in the ghettos of the United States commonly referred to as "the project" illustrate this type of slum. In the United States these residences at least begin with some semblance of amenities: running water in each unit, electricity, heat, and indoor facilities. However, the cheap construction often turns these supposed amenities into jokes as more and more time elapses without the needed maintenance.[22]

A less desirable slum town would be illustrated by the "townships" of South Africa. It is a separate and distinct community from the city, usually an island town within the larger city or existing on its outskirts. These areas are deliberately planned to enforce strict apartheid. In some cases they may not be characterized by the extreme physical squallor typical of some slums. Rather the blight is more social and moral because of the social isolation and psychological alienation it fosters.

A final type of slum needs to be emphasized. It is distinct from anything mentioned above because it is not a residence or dwelling in the sense of "housing." Perhaps it is not a slum in the strictest sense. It is more a condition and a way of life. The mobile, unsheltered squatters who live by the millions on the streets of the major cities of India such as Calcutta and Bombay illustrate this slum style. They dwell singly or in family groups—sometimes generation after generation—on the streets, subject to the elements as much as any unsheltered animal. They shift from one place to another, victimized by the authorities, their fellow countrymen, the weather, and their own ignorance. They eke out one of the most pathetic and deplorable forms of existence known to humanity. Everything any other human being does—eat, sleep, urinate, defecate, rest, make love, have babies, die—these people do on the streets of the city.[23]

Another form of mobile slum life-style is illustrated by the traditional waterfront "floating slums." These people usually at least have some shelter over their heads, but they suffer immeasurably from the heavy rains and winds when the storms come. They live an extremely vulnerable life-style and often do not survive the ravages either of nature or society.[24]

Not all of the urban poor live in slums, it needs to be emphasized strongly. Many live in transitional areas we sometimes call the inner city. These communities are not slums, though they may become so in time. Often the people who live here are not the absolute poor. However, because they are unskilled, they are often underemployed. They live on the border line of poverty, woefully below the level of the average middle class or even lower middle class. They oscillate back and forth from the poverty level in a rhythm of frustration which in time takes its toll in terms of self-image and motivation.[25]

Theological and Missiological Implications

The whole problem of urban poverty raises profound questions for the church and the Christian world mission today. Some of these questions are: How do we come to terms with the fact that "the poor" in the Bible—both in the Old and the New Testaments—is a significant theological frame of reference? How do we deal with that solemn fact in light of the middle-class orientation, if not captivity, of the North Atlantic church (especially Protestant) which has shaped the nature and style of the church worldwide?

Moving from theology to sociology, how do we interpret the significance of the fact that the whole world is becoming urbanized, in light of the rural mysticism which has colored if not controlled the theology and mentality of the American Protestant (especially Baptist) churches? How do we come to grips with the fact that the Third World (which we are now more accurately beginning to call the "Three-Fourths World") is becoming as urbanized as the North Atlantic world but without an indigenous, grass roots economic revolution which leaves them with all the problems of urban life but few of the amenities? What do we do with the fact that these "Three-Fourths World" cities are largely poor because they have a majority population which is poor—much of it hard-core?

How do we address the reality that in this "Three-Fourths World" Christianity is growing much more rapidly than in its more traditional home of the North Atlantic world? Does this church of the poor have anything to say to us? Is God saying something to us through the emerging worldwide church of the poor? If so, what? That is the theological question! If so, what do we do about it? That is the missiological question![26]

"The Poor" as a Significant Biblical Frame of Reference

Nothing is clearer in Scripture than the fact that the God of the Bible is the champion of the poor, the downtrodden, the exploited. All one has to do, if he or she is not convinced, is to consult the some 300 Old Testament references to the poor, translated from a half-dozen different basic terms for "the poor." When we add related terms such as "the stranger," "the fatherless," and "widows" (which are usually used to describe a context of poverty), the number of references becomes almost astronomical.

Two ways in which the Old Testament makes significant reference to the poor are in the passages which reveal the biblical sensitivity to the plight of the poor and in the many condemnations of the oppressors who exploit the poor. An example of the former is in the many legal provisions and ethical admonitions illustrated in the principle of gleaning (for example, Lev. 19:9; 23:22). An example of the latter is in the many woes of judgment pronounced by the prophets because of the oppression of the poor (Isa. 3:14,15; 10:1-4; Amos 4:1-3; 5:11-12, and many others).

The most scathing denunciations were reserved for those who were guilty of the two most grievous sins: the turning away from the worship of the only true God and the oppression of the poor. Ezekiel speaks of the two in the same breath when he condemns the person who "oppresses the poor and needy, commits robbery, does not restore the pledge, lifts up his eyes to the idols, commits abomination" (18:12).

The New Testament is just as decisive in its reference to the poor. The whole historical and cultural context of the incarnation—the humble circumstance chosen by God for his manifestation in the flesh—has significant theological implications. The self-understanding of Jesus is significantly linked to the poor. In his opening declaration of his identity and ministry in the synagogue in Nazareth, he quoted Isaiah 61 and said emphatically that "This day is this scripture fulfilled in your ears" (4:21, KJV):

> The Spirit of the Lord is upon me,/because he has anointed me to preach good news to the poor./He has sent me to proclaim release to the captives . . . to set at liberty those who are oppressed (Luke 4:18).

In his teaching he not only condemned those who oppressed the poor (Mark 12:40), but he made a suggestively startling and frightening application of how we treat the poor to our eternal destination. Two classic examples of this one are the parable of the rich man and Lazarus (Luke 16:19-31) and his powerful sermon on "the least of these" (Matt. 25:31-46).

In the growth of the apostolic church at that crucial time when the gospel was opening to the Gentiles, a significant and lasting decision was made. In Paul's account of this, he emphasized the common grace that was given to both the Jewish and the Gentile community. Peter, James, and John gave to Paul and Barnabas the right hand of fellowship. They would continue to minister to the circumcision, and Paul and Barnabas were free to go to the Gentiles. But one ultimate and final stipulation remains—that they "remember the poor." The ancient hallmark of the identification of God's people—circumcision —is expendable. But not the poor! They must never be forgotten! Paul's rejoinder to the admonition to remember the poor was, "Which very thing I was eager to do." Paul's devotion to the poor saints at Jerusalem and the admonition of James concerning treatment of the poor (2:1-7,15-16; 5:1-6) give the touch of finality to the church's identification with the poor in the New Testament.

Why does the Bible make such a point of the poor? If the gospel is for everyone, why single out the poor in this special way? The reason is that if we do not make a special effort to include them, they get left out. They have no power. They are the outcasts, the disenfranchised, the nobodies of the earth. They do not count. Poverty is like a disease. It carries a stigma. It is bad enough to go hungry and to have nothing—to see those you love go hungry and be humiliated by the absence of the basic amenities of life. But the greatest stigma is the psychological one—the total estrangement, the dehumanization, the loss of dignity, and a sense of worthlessness that no creature made in God's image should be forced to feel.

Inspiring Attempts Thus Far

It is easy to castigate ourselves concerning the urban poor. To say we have done nothing and are doing nothing is not even honest. It is common to hear such statements as: "We don't know how to relate to the city" . . . "Nobody is doing anything in the city" . . . "Our seminaries are not training anyone for the city." The above indictments may be true as they relate to the inner city and the transitional areas of marginal poverty and the slum areas of hard-core poverty. But even here our masochistic attitudes are not entirely justified.

From New Testament times, there has always been the city church. The cathedral has always been a place to which the poor as well as the rich could come. For many centuries the church itself was poor. Despite its growing acceptability and respectibility in the Middle Ages, the ministry of the church to the poor is legendary. The missionary movement has witnessed extensive ministries of healing and education as well as evangelism to the urban poor. The Salvation Army with its theology and missiology of "soup, soap, and salvation" institutionalized this ministry to the poor. Since then rescue missions and a thousand other ministries have carried many to work with the urban poor. From such notable illustrations as the great Japanese Christian Toyohiko Kagawa who went to live in the slums of Tokyo to the dramatic urban-industrial mission programs which began in England and America and spread Eastward to Asia, there has been a decisive witness of the church among the urban poor in recent years.

Denominations have had a growing sensitivity in this area, and many creative efforts have been expended in the inner city. Theological schools have been adapting their curriculum to make ministerial students sensitive to the needs of the urban poor. For over fifteen years Golden Gate Baptist Theological Seminary has taken some of its class settings to the inner city of San Francisco and Oakland. Deeply committed theological professors such as George W. Webber in New York and Ray Bakke in Chicago have raised their families in the inner city. Inspiring churches such as the Allen Temple Baptist Church of East Oakland,[27] the Bronx Baptist Church of New York,[28] and the Assembly of God Church of Calcutta, India,[29] are famous for the way they have deeply identified with the urban poor. And they symbolize a host of other churches similarly involved. Roman Catholic leaders in Latin America—nationals and missionaries—have cast their lot with the masses in an amazing and inspiring solidarity with the poor. We cannot rightly say, "Nobody knows what to do"; "nobody is doing anything"; "nobody cares."

The Remaining Challenge

Though there are many who care and many who are deeply involved, the number is far too few and the effort is far too limited. The needs are so massive and they multiply in such staggering proportions every year that the challenge has become all but overwhelming.

It will take more than just more people and more ministries, however; it will take a reordering of the priorities of the church and the Christian world mission. This reordering of priorities, however, will come only with an authentic renewal of the people of God.

It does not come within the purpose of this chapter to deal with strategy. However, no discussion of the church and the urban poor can be complete without reference to some of the guiding principles that must be the basis of any meaningful mission strategy of the church among the urban poor.

The greatest problem of the past has been the paternalism which has characterized ministry to the poor. In both Africa and America, this has been the case. Ministry can no longer be "for" or "to"—it must be "with." The poor are doubly humiliated when those who profess to care for them and who believe they are sent to serve among them do not bring them into partnership with them. A condescending and patronizing attitude which is unwilling to listen to the poor in terms of what is best for their community is irresponsible and can no longer be tolerated.

The problem next in magnitude is the lack of a holistic ideology and methodology in urban ministry among the poor. There has been in the past too much of a tendency to be either only traditionally evangelistic or completely social-action oriented. What is needed is both presence and proclamation, or better still a vital proclamation of the gospel from a deeply involved incarnational presence with a profoundly caring social consciousness.

Fundamental to this is the life of the Christian community itself. The fellowship of the body and the liturgical life of the people of God must furnish the deepest driving force in any urban ministry among the poor. The power of the Word of God studied, proclaimed, shared, and lived will be the renewing source which makes a difference in people's lives. The vital presence, leadership, and guidance of the Holy Spirit will give power and purpose to people in the midst of the challenge of the adverse social context in which the urban poor have to cope—whether it is the oppressively humiliating pressures from above or the morally corrupting pressures from below.

Out of this spiritual foundation and life-affirming reservoir of Christian caring and support will come the needed structures of renewal and the guidelines for strategy to be implemented at all levels: intercommunity, ecumenical, denominational, congregational, communal, personal.

The Meaning of the Church of the Poor

One of the most significant events of the twentieth century is the phenomenal growth of Christianity in the Third (Three-Fourths) World. With Europe's Christian population and influence declining

and North America's holding its own, the most significant growth
of Christianity is in Africa, Asia, and Latin America. The strength of
Christianity is shifting from its historic bastion in the Northern tier
to the Southern tier of nations. The major exception to this is Korea.
However, the significant growth of the church in Korea further
accents the fact that the most impressive expansion of the gospel is
outside its traditional power base in the North Atlantic nations.

The significance of this reality for the church and Christian world
mission today is in the fact that the emerging majority Christian
population in the world is in those countries where the majority of
the population is poor. We are coming full circle back to the apostolic era in which most churches and Christians were poor. Another
aspect of this historical-sociological-ecclesiological full circle is the
fact that the New Testament church was an urban church, and the
demographic reality of our emerging future will make the modern
church an urban church (by and large). This means the emerging
numerical and spiritual strength of world Christianity will be more
and more concentrated in churches constituted of the urban poor.[30]

It is true that America has long had a church of the urban poor.
Perhaps this has been best symbolized in the vast number of storefront churches in the inner cities, especially of the larger metropolitan centers. However, though these churches may constitute a
majority in the slum and depressed areas of the inner city (sometimes
several in one block) in terms of the nation—even the larger metropolitan region—they are a minority. The emerging phenomenon
in Africa, Asia, and Latin America is in stark contrast to this. In these
areas of the underdeveloped and developing nations, the church of
the urban poor is becoming the majority church (and in many cases
it already is). To establish a vital and meaningful solidarity and
partnership with this emerging church of the urban poor is one of
the greatest challenges facing the mainstream, strongly middle-class
denominations of the North-Atlantic world.

This socioecclesial challenge is compounded by another reality
which is religioecclesial. This is the fact that most of the astounding
growth of church in the Three-Fourths World is represented by what
some are calling the "Fourth Force" in the modern history of the

church. In distinction from Roman Catholicism, Eastern Orthodoxy, and mainstream Protestantism, this Fourth Force is largely Pentecostal. It is orthodox, but its theological emphasis and its communal and liturgical style are charismatic, which has made it separate to a large degree for both internal reasons (the desire for freedom of expression) and external reasons (unacceptance by mainstream historic groups). However, because the growth has been so phenomenal and the emerging strength is so resourceful, it has become a force to be reckoned with. Because of the reality of this emerging church of the urban poor, traditional Christian bodies must find a way to link hands with them both in terms of fellowship and mission (because the two ultimately cannot be separated).

Roman Catholics and the more liberal ecumenical Protestant bodies, even the Eastern Orthodox community, have been more effective in this regard than the more conservative Protestant bodies such as the Baptists. This is a double challenge because next to the Pentecostals the Baptists are the most rapidly expanding group in the world. Of course, it is understandable that in some situations this is difficult. For example, when an African independent group has crossed the boundary from indigenous to syncretistic or when a Latin American Pentecostal group is divisive in an overbearing emphasis upon the gifts, this unity may not be possible. However, the acceptance into the World Council of Churches of the Kimbanguist Church of Zaire and the Brazil for Christ Church is evidence that it can happen.

The growing admiration and respect from the world Christian community which has been accorded the Yoido Island Central Full Gospel Church in Seoul, Korea, the fastest-growing and largest church in the world and one with an amazing quality and stability, is a breakthrough in this much needed area of mutual recognition. Although South Korea is much better off economically than much of the Three-Fourths World—though the church in Korea may be more lower or emerging middle class than poor (certainly in the hard-core sense)—South Korea is still a developing nation. Church growth there, especially reflected in this phenomenal church and others, represents something new in the history of Christianity.

The problems of our emerging urban world are so vast and the threat of non-Christian forces so great that it behooves all authentic Christian groups as never before to present a united front in our world witness. And what is more, traditional church groups have a great deal to learn from this new Christian force on how to establish rapport with and how to reach for Christ the vast multitudes of the poor in the vastly expanding cities of the world.

The emerging church of the urban poor is forcing us to see God's view of the poor—exactly opposite of the world's. We look upon the poor with pity. Jesus said, "Blessed are the poor" (Matt. 5:3). The believing poor have nowhere to look but to God, and in the Christian faith the urban poor are recovering their sense of worth as made in the image of God and as redeemed by the love of Christ. Liberation begins in the heart.

This liberation, moreover, flows further into the fellowship of faith and into the community of the urban poor. Like the poor who have long gathered in their urban storefronts in America, the Christian communities are proliferating among the urban poor in the wake of an impressive advance of the gospel and are gathering in "shop churches" and in "house churches" in all major areas of the world. In Latin America the Basic Christian Communities, a renewal form of the church, are growing in number and influence. With their strong emphasis upon the relation of worship to mission, they have been able to relate faith to life and find new hope in the face of oppression and conditions of poverty. They have become a model for the church in Africa and Asia, and their influence is now beginning to be felt in Europe and North America.

If this and similar movements continue to make an impact around the world, the church worldwide will be able to enter significantly into solidarity and partnership with the poor. Out of this can come a more united Christian faith in the world, a deeper sharing of spiritual and material resources, and a force which will make for change both in the communities of the urban poor and in the oppressive structures of urban society responsible for this poverty.[31] May God's people in this awesome and promising hour unite to meet this challenge.

Notes

1. See *World Development Report,* (Washington: World Bank, 1978); also *Christian Witness to the Urban Poor,* The Thailand Report on the Urban Poor, Consultation on World Evangelization, Pattaya, Thailand, June 16-17, 1980 (Wheaton: Lausanne Committee for World Evangelization, 1980), p. 5.

2. *Christian Witness to the Urban Poor,* p. 7-8.

3. Ibid., p. 8.

4. Ibid., p. 7.

5. Ibid. See also Thomas J. Courtney, "Mission to the Urban Poor," *Urban Mission,* Nov. 1983, pp. 17-24.

6. *Christian Witness to the Urban Poor,* p. 7. See also Francis M. DuBose, "Cities Aren't All Alike: The Common and Contrasting Urban Context of the Christian Global Mission," *Urban Mission,* Jan. 1984, pp. 18-22.

7. *Christian Witness to the Urban Poor,* pp. 6-7. See also Francis M. DuBose, "Slums: Worldwide Problem," *The Commission,* Aug. 1970, pp. 3-4.

8. *Christian Witness to the Urban Poor,* p. 6.

9. V. T. Rajshekar Shetty, *Apartheid in India* (Bangalore: Dalit Action Committee, 1978), p. 8.

10. *Christian Witness to the Urban Poor,* p. 5.

11. Benjamin Tonna, *Gospel for Cities: A Socio-Theology of Urban Ministry,* trans. William E. Jerman (Maryknoll: Orbis Books, 1982), pp. 40-44. See also DuBose, 1984, pp. 18-20.

12. See Tonna, 1982. See also M. A. McGee, *The Urbanization Process in the Third World* (London: G. Bell and Sons, Ltd., 1971).

13. See Tonna, 1982 and McGee, 1971. See also DuBose, 1984, pp. 18-20.

14. Ibid.

15. See *Christian Witness to the Urban Poor,* pp. 5-6. See also Aprodico A. Laquian, *Slums are for People* (Manila: University of the Philippines, 1969).

16. See DuBose, 1970, p. 2.

17. Ibid.

18. Ibid., p. 3.

19. Ibid. See also *Christian Witness to the Urban Poor,* p. 6.

20. Ibid.

21. DuBose, 1970, p. 3.

22. Ibid. pp. 3-4.

23. Ibid., p. 4.

24. Ibid.

25. Much of the above description on slums comes from the author's firsthand investigation of slum areas in Africa, India, Southeast Asia, the Middle East, and Latin America under supervision of knowledgeable persons involved in urban work in the cities of these countries and areas of the world. It is also based upon the author's 25 years of direct involvement in urban mission in Detroit, San Francisco, and Oakland. Other bibliographic sources furnishing information and ideas are: Marshall B. Clinard, *Slums and Community Development* (New York: The Free Press, 1966); Michael Harrington, *The Other America: Poverty*

in the United States (New York: The Macmillan Co., 1962); David R. Hunter, *The Slums: Challenge and Response* (New York: The Free Press, 1964). Though the information in these studies is now dated, the studies remain definitive in terms of treatment of the phenomenon of slums.

26. See Orlando Costas, *Christ Outside the Gate: Mission Beyond Christendom* (Maryknoll: Orbis Books, 1982).

27. See G. Willis Bennett, *Guidelines for Effective Urban Church Ministry,* Based on a Case Study of Allen Temple Baptist Church (Nashville: Broadman Press, 1983).

28. See Walker Knight, "The Church at the Bronx, New York," *Seven Beginnings: The Human Touch in Starting Churches* (Atlanta: Home Mission Board, SBC, 1976) pp. 105-131.

29. See Douglas Wood, *The Compassionate Touch* (Carol Stream: Creation House, 1977).

30. See Julio De Santa Ana, *Toward a Church of the Poor* (Maryknoll, N.Y.: Orbis Books, 1981). See also Walbert Buhlmann, *The Coming of the Third Church* (Maryknoll N.Y.: Orbis Books, 1976).

31. See Sergio Torres and John Eagleson, eds., *The Challenge of Basic Christian Communities.* (Maryknoll: Orbis Books, 1981). See also Courtney, pp. 17-24.

4

Evangelization of the World's Cities

Raymond J. Bakke

Broadly speaking, we can classify the three billion non-Christians of the world in two categories: (1) the geographically distant unreached peoples, and (2) the culturally distant unreached peoples.[1] The *geographically distant* unreached peoples are those who are the legitimate focus of traditional (overseas) missionary efforts. These include the last mountain tribe or jungle village. To reach them requires the bridging of geographical distance *and* cultural distance. By all accounts, there is still a great and continuing need for the traditional foreign mission in today's world. Fortunately, however, the younger churches of the two-thirds non-Western world have picked up this challenge and are organizing their own mission agencies. The church and the mission is now a global reality. We can celebrate that today.

The *culturally distant* unreached peoples include millions of persons who are not geographically distant. They are found in the huge and rapidly growing cities of the world. Even if they live right next door to us, they often remain outside the vision and evangelistic mission of our traditional evangelical churches because they are somehow culturally different from the dominant culture of the congregation. They will not be reached for Jesus Christ unless existing churches become multicultural by intention or unless user-friendly churches are started by and for them.

For two thousand years the church has possessed the Great Commission to go, preach, baptize, and disciple every individual, group, or people in the world. But in our day, we can see the commission in a totally new light, for now we know where to find the nations or peoples of the world and the direction in which they are moving. Like giant magnets, Third World cities are pulling people out of rural poverty in hope of new opportunities.

The most significant inflation impacting our world today is not the inflation of our currencies but the inflation of our expectations. Elfan Rees has called this "the century of homeless man."[2] The reality is that apart from the known ten to fifteen million involuntary migrants we normally call refugees in the world, millions more are voluntary migrants and *de facto* refugees trying to find their way towards or within the large cities. The United States is being very much implicated and impacted by the global population explosion and what University of Chicago demographer Phillip Hauser calls "the population implosion i.e., the rapid growth of peoples in confined spaces, which we might call the pressure-cooker syndrome."

Large cities assault the sensitivies of many middle-class Christians. The very image of city may conjure up negative feelings of noise, dirt, crime, or threat. Early urbanologists like Park and Burgess also thought this. For them, as for many today, the rural, familial, and pastoral is normative; the city is a deviant pattern or social pathology which, like cancer, keeps encroaching upon us. Where such a view of cities prevails, it is difficult to inform and motivate Christians about the contemporary opportunities of urban mission.

As difficult as it may be for many to believe, most new urban dwellers choose to migrate there and very often they find it much more hopeful than the rural or small-town environments they left. Not only have they found new access to education, jobs, political involvement, and social status, many are encountering Jesus Christ in the city because of the creative and compassionate ministries of thousands of urban churches and mission agencies.

We could wish it were in the Bible, but George Bernard Shaw said, "You see things; and you say, 'Why?' But I dream things that never were; and I say, 'Why not?' " For many people cities are a problem, even a disaster. But for those of us who love the challenge of world mission and evangelism, cities represent profound new opportunities.

The Significance of Cities

The *demographic* significance of cities has been described elsewhere in this volume. Demographics has to do with numbers. Put simply, most large cities in the developing world will double within the next ten to fifteen years. The 240 world class cities of December 1982 will increase to 500 by the year 2000.[3]

When you read in *Popline,* or any number of population studies, that the world population grows at the rate of six million persons per month, try to visualize that number to feel its reality. That is *two* new Chicagos a month on planet earth or a new Chicago and a new Los Angeles every single month. The urban numbers are staggering.

Mexico City was projected to reach eighteen million by January 1984. This one city is growing at the rate of 6.2 percent per year. Three and two-tenths percent is due to the birth rate; the remaining 3.0 percent is due to migration. While the cities of the USA have a median age of about 30, Mexico City's median age is 14.2, meaning that nine million babies and children live in that one city. Many cities of South America, Africa, and Asia are developing similar profiles. Thus, it can be said that while Mexico City is the oldest city in our hemisphere; it is also the largest and the youngest. The challenges to mission cry out to us.

Cairo, the largest city in Africa, spreads faster in acres than the land being reclaimed by the Aswan High Dam. Lagos is 25 percent unemployed and 25 percent underemployed. Nairobi grows at nearly 9 percent per year, but the numbers on crime rise faster.

Most Americans probably perceive South America as largely rural, dominated by the Andes and Amazon. Yet that continent is 64 percent urban now and rapidly becoming more urban and industrial.[4]

Global urbanization, moreover, is probably part of an even larger worldwide phenomena—the Asianization of the world. Nearly 50 of every 100 babies born in the world are Asian. In fact, by the year 2000, the population of Asia alone will be almost 4 billion persons.

It took six centuries (AD 800-1400) for the world to shift from the Mediterranean center to a North Atlantic center. Since 1500 we have been a North Atlantic perimeter world. Now that historic reality is passing away. The Pacific perimeter, driven by huge populations, expanding technologies, and phenomenal resources will be the center of the world symbolized by a large ring of conurbations or massive interconnected metropolitan centers.[5]

Cities, then, are not only demographically significant because of their large numbers of people, they are *prophetically* significant because they are the engines of social, political, and cultural changes impacting the whole world. In brief, if you want to know what the whole world will look like in twenty years, look at the large cities today.

A generation ago, urbanologists defined cities by their *forms* or structures, such as size, density of heterogeneity.[6] Recently, under the influence of cultural anthropology and social psychology, they have defined cities by *functions* or roles. This is a helpful designation because it enables us to track the differences between urban (as place) and urbanization (as process).

When Johnny Carson comes on TV and is projected to rural America every night, he brings his urban friends, values, language, music, and products to sell. He becomes a cultural John the Baptist promoting what we might crassly call "the Los-Angelization of rural America." Cities, then, are giant stereophonic amplifiers significant for evangelism not only because of the huge numbers of people who live and work there, but because their influence often grows even when their population declines. One cannot escape the city.

A third reason for the primacy of large cities in the world mission of the church today is what we might label strategy. The very diversity of and linkages between cities multiply evangelization results far beyond our initial efforts. The "World Class City" designation identifies characteristics of large cities: they have over one million persons (form or structure), and they have international influence (function or roles). Thus this definition tries to capture both sides of the urbanological debate and at the same time conceptualize the significance of cities for world evangelization.

In the mid-1960s two marvelously significant legislative changes passed Congress and profoundly altered our country. First, the Civil

Rights Act of 1964 abolished *de jure* racism in our domestic life. The second piece of legislation, passed in 1965, was equally profound but less well known. It changed our immigration laws, abolishing racial quotas for persons seeking to enter the United States from the outside. It means that Asians, Africans, and Latins have larger numbers, Europeans smaller. In a word, Chicago—formerly an ethnically European city—is rapidly Asianizing. Houston public schools are now 80 percent Black, Hispanic, and Asian. Cities are internationalizing. "Boat people" from South East Asia, hitherto unaccessible to the gospel, are finding Christ in Chicago. The same experiences and phenomena describe the new mission institutes in nearly every other major city in the world at home and abroad. We can now talk concretely about the global mission of the local church in ways mission executives never dreamed about even a few years ago.

Obviously, if the local urban churches at home need to do the very same things the foreign local churches need to do, then new challenges and problems emerge. Everything the foreign missionaries learned about cross-cultural ministry are now needed by pastors and church staffs at home. Home and foreign mission agencies will obviously need to share resources and begin to plan joint strategies that impact both ends of international, immigrant, and migrant streams. There are obvious implications for seminary and other training programs also. Environments are never neutral. No foreign mission employs staff without contextualized cultural and linguistic studies. Clearly, that which we have done for Sao Paulo, Brazil, we need to do for Saint Paul, Minnesota. As we prepared for Medelleín, so for Miami; as for Caracas, so for Chicago.

Having established the legitimate significance of large city evangelization, let us identify some of the clear challenges these cities present to us as evangelicals. What follows is by no means exhaustive, only suggestive.

The Challenges of Large City Evangelization

The Structural Challenge

Cities are not simply loose collections of individual people. Cities package people, often in predictable ways. Like the human body, cities are systems. One's neural system is attached to the skeletal and circulatory systems. The totality of systems is the real you. Injury or change in one system impacts the whole. "Sounds obvious," you say. Cities, too, are ecological systems. Chicago, like Sao Paulo and Bombay, has an "industrial heart." These cities are dirty, noisy, smokestack cities. That is their corporate personality and that is why some people come to live in these places who would for instance never go to San Francisco.

San Francisco, like Rio de Janeiro or Paris, is a cultural city at heart. The chief products are ideas, fashions, or trends. This attracts very different groups of avant-garde folks and their ethos is very different.

Washington, DC, Brasilia, or New Delhi could be designated administrative cities because their chief product is power or influence. People often live schizophrenically within them. They are headquarters cities like Nairobi or Miami. People are *in* those cities but not of them in rather obvious ways.

To a mission strategist or a new church developer, Chicago and other "smokestack cities" could be linked worldwide. Ministry models in one will probably work in similar cities abroad even while they would not work in Boston. Los Angeles and New York are commercial cities, and they also have their counterparts abroad. Mexico City, Lima, or London combine their multiple roles so we could call them primary cities. They are really city-states. Jerusalem, Soweto, Rome, or Berlin are symbolic cities.

Cities have structured, corporate personalities. You cannot, or at least should not, assume you can franchize evangelism models for all cities everywhere because they are profoundly different corporate structures. Not only are cities macro or large structures, they also constitute micro or small structures as well. For example, Warren and Warren classify each of Chicago's seventy-seven different neighborhoods in six different paradigms.

Integral
Parochial
Diffuse
Stepping-stone
Transitory
Anomic[7]

Each has its own distinctive communication pattern, both within and without. Knowing this can make or break a local ministry.

Why would urban missionaries or pastors who spent years mastering the grammatical paradigms of Hebrew and Greek or studying the psychological paradigms of personality types then not study the contextual paradigms of the city? This should be done in order to custom-build effective urban congregations appropriate to the structures of the urban context.

Cities are systems and structures just like families and persons. They can be studied, understood, and communicated with in appropriate, compassionate ways. But like complex persons, large cities usually will not yield to our paternalistic, simplistic blitzkriegs. Urban structures are a new challenge for most of us.[8]

The Pluralistic Challenge

Fundamentally, rural life is generalized and urban life is specialized. That is a very basic difference between our contrasting environments. In a rural area, we know everybody and generally relate to our woodpiles (heat) and our gardens (food) in personal ways. We are emotionally invested in life at each frequency.

The city changes all that. We cannot possibly invest emotionally in a million personal relationships. In the city we choose our relationships and save our emotions for special causes. We do not talk in elevators because intuitively we know it would invade our neighbors' space. The closer people live to us in cities, the less we communicate because of the psychological principle of overload.[9] The implications for the polychromed existence we call urban life-style and, therefore, for evangelism are critical. People do not open doors, do not know neighbors, and often do not list or answer phones. Yet they break out into different and often bizzare life-styles and value systems. That is surely a challenge to evangelistic strategy and new church development.

It would appear that urban churches should develop specialized approaches congruent with urban personality profiles. Look at growing urban churches and they may be ministering to some fundamental underlying realities. For example, many urban folk are existential or experience-oriented people. They go like bees from experience to experience. They will drive fifty miles across the city to a congregational experience that is existentially relevant. Charismatic churches are proliferating everywhere in cities to reach people like this.

A second personality profile we might call relational. Relational persons hunger for a few intense, stable, even familial relationships. They gravitate to churches that promise *not* to grow very large, often to house or single cell churches. They want church to compensate for the loss of family. If they hunger for an absent father, they may gravitate to a cell structure with an authoritarian pastor/leader. If they hunger for surrogate brothers and sisters, they may gravitate to communal body-life structured churches. Here again the urban church is asked to specialize and to provide compensation for the victims of American dreams that do not come true, families that were not secure or whole.

Yet another urban personality group might be the task or goal-directed type. These people join churches like they join clubs to ski, climb mountains, or parachute out of airplanes. They seek action and challenge—high commitment, task-oriented urban churches grab them. Then there are the artists who may be oral or visual. The oral groups live with sounds. They cannot jog without their music. It is the way they feed their psyche and put boundaries around their existence. Cities are full of people like this. The urban visuals are so often assaulted by the aesthetics of traditional church architecture, decor, and other physical elements that they cannot hear what we say.

To highlight the significance of artistic unreached urban peoples, think again for a few moments about Mexico City. Clearly, the dominant communicator of ideas in the past generation was the national artist Diego Rivera, a socialist whose murals adore the national palace and the university library. Combining images from Mayan and Aztec cultures with Picasso-like techniques, he worked in paint and stone. The power of his communication across social class lines has been phenomenal. Incidentally, Carlos Chavez, the founder of the Mexican Symphony, used the same approach as Rivera to create a national music for Mexico.

Now you might think that every mission in Mexico would deploy staffs of creative artists for their evangelism strategies congruent with this uniquely Mexican, urban art mystique. The sad reality is, however, that missions are still handing out tracts and trying to force programmatic responses on the church.

Jakarta and Mexico City are just two of the many cities where art and drama may be the most significant mission media. Obviously, our mission agencies at home and abroad are hardly ready for these challenges to our traditional denominational musicology and middle-class distrust of art.

The pluralism of the city goes beyond the personality types. In most urban communities, you see the various profiles or clienteles.

Business	Politician
Commercial	Night People
Public aid	Commuters
Ethnic	Middle Class
Institutionalized	Upper Class
Deviant	Lower Class
Derelicts	Drop Outs
Theater	Migrants
Student	Elderly
International	Immigrants
Professional	

Each of these groups may include thousands. Many persons fit in more than one category, of course. Each group may be a kind of subculture with life patterns very different from the congregation in that same neighborhood.

A multiple staff in many large cities should work twenty-four-hour shifts like police and hospitals do. The four-to-midnight pastoral styles and programs (like the local police beat strategies and staffs) would look very different from the midnight-to-eight or eight-to-four programs. This is so obvious it should not even need mention. But it is amazing how few churches or mission strategists plan around the concept that the urban clock runs twenty-four hours; and churches, like grocery stores and other institutions, must respond or adapt, die, or depart.

Pluralism threatens us all, especially when we have psychological needs to feel big—as most white Americans do right now—in a world of mostly yellow, brown, and black folks. Large cities make minorities of us all and tend to make pastors or evangelists feel very marginal. In the rural area or the county seat, we had the visibility of building and program to counter our psychological insecurities and reaffirm our spiritual call to ministry. In the city we usually have neither. We need a different theological value system and a strong commitment to the kingdom of God to compensate for the little we seem to be accomplishing.

The Challenge to Leadership

Generally speaking, for missions that went to Latin America and Africa (less in Asia), the Bible school became the normative way to develop pastors and evangelists. Even where seminaries emerged representing the upgrading of leadership standards, most students came from the small towns to train for ministry. The small-town pastor and area missionary may well have been the most competent and best-trained persons in the region. To be like them, young men and women followed the educational path to the city where the Bible school was located.[10]

Meanwhile, the young men and women of city churches more often choose other vocational options on the fast track into the professions. They become physicans, business persons, or academicians. Failing this, they may prepare for ministry which in most Third World cities is a low-status vocation.

The ripple effect continues when the rural ministry student graduates from the Bible school and then, for a variety of reasons, takes an urban pastorate. Unless a rather radical reorientation takes place, this new young leader will pastor a rural church in the city. These pastors will distrust and be threatened by the upper classes and increasingly be aware of their own limitations. Most will not study or understand their new host cities and live as aliens in them, just like the missionaries who taught them do. More often than not, the pastors compensate for the growing marginality they feel by resorting to rather authoritarian and noncollaborative styles of ministry.

Meanwhile, the highest single group of immigrants to most cities, especially in Latin America, is teenage girls.[11] They come with and without husbands because the city is more open to them and their new aspirations for education, employment, and liberation than the countryside. Imagine a young ex-rural couple now living in a Brazilian Favela (their name is "Legion"). Each day they rise and go to work—he to a low-skilled outdoor construction job where he works with other unreconstructed ex-villagers who just happen to live in the city now. His wife dresses up, goes downtown to the heart of the city, works in an office, and learns computer languages. Later, at home she meets the same village expectations of her husband—who assumes she is and always will be the woman he married.

If this couple goes to church, Pentecostal or Baptist, they will probably encounter the ex-rural preacher who will blame her for strains in the marriage. In fact the same pastor will probably be so threatened by her new world of awareness that he will be even less likely to enlist her gifts for church leadership than he might have been in the rural or small town back home. Is it any wonder that cities challenge the leadership of the church and the mission that establishes it?

The urban ministry tool kit is quite different than the traditional one most of us got at seminary. Most pastors and missionaries give lip service to our role as the assistant ministers of the church in which the members are the real ministers. This reminds us of yet another challenge of the city to the church and its mission.

The Challenge of "GO Structured" Ministries

The traditional church gathers people, usually all at once, in ever-expanding sanctuaries and in settings where the minister's role, authority, and competence are very clear. Urban people, like most folks everywhere, have three sets of networks that produce our personal identities. We can call them *biological*—those people related to us; *geographical*—those people who live near us; *vocational*—those people who work with us. In a rural area the first two are especially visible. If people ask us *who* we are, we tell them who we are related to and where we live. In a city, however, ask ten people *who* they are and they will tell you *what* they do. "I'm a lawyer, teacher, secretary." That is not who they are, of course. That is what they do, but that *is* the primary identity of most urban people.[12]

If this is so, pastors should probably visit urban homes less than urban offices and factories, and many do. In fact by appointment they visit the members' place of work, be it bank, school, or factory to help the members define their ministry including their circle of influence for evangelism and pastoral care. Many urban mission leaders or pastors know next to nothing about the technical worlds of their members. We who in the rural areas could use down-home, farm, or appropriate illustrations now find ourselves less and less able to help our members reach their worlds for Jesus, the world of their primary spiritual and vocational identities. In fact urban evangelical pastors often adopt the medieval church view of work which says there really is a hierarchy of work. What you do during the day is useful, but your real work is at the church in our busy program. Note how different this is from Luther who taught us that we could serve God *in* our vocations or Calvin who taught us we could serve God *with* our vocations.

Why should the urban business leader who is struggling with his or her identity and role come to a sanctuary where one's real or imagined identities are stripped away? Is it not evident why so few men who experience the city life as normally emasculating are less than enthusiastic about our churches? On the other hand, because so many male pastors and missionaries exude decisiveness and strength, we attract women in abundance. Paul knew, as most of us know, that it isn't just the Spirit of Christ that draws the urban women to the churches (see 1 Cor. 15). In many ways, the city challenges our most fundamental assumptions and habits of ministry when they don't work (and even when they do).

The Challenge of Different Values

When God wanted to communicate, he did not wire the universe for stereo or write of his love in vapor trails. Neither was Jesus a commuter, living with his family in a nice community while he tracked daily into the bad neighborhoods. It is rather amazing how in the name of the incarnate Christ who "became flesh and dwelt among us" (John 1:14), we church and mission leaders resort to impersonal ministries, crusades, or blitzes as compensation for our own unwillingness to invest our lives and families in the neighborhoods where the people we serve actually live.

Headquarter mission ministries are the bane of large cities everywhere. Christians commute into headquarters which *use* the urban space, banks, airports, post offices, highways, and other cultural benefits without either directly investing in those centers or ministering to them.[13]

Nehemiah confronted a typical urban reality in his time. Jerusalem was a ruin and no one wanted to live inside the walls. So this creative Persian Jewish layman got a government grant and leave of absence for the rebuilding of a model city's program and opted for a new strategy. He asked families and villages to tithe *people* who would move into, colonize, and rebuild the city from within. The people responded and ordained or commissioned those who were willing to live in Jerusalem (see Neh. 11:1-2).

When will we Americans learn that we can no more bomb cities with programs of evangelization from without than we could bomb Vietnam into submission and victory. The Vietnam analogy is deliberate. It was as much the technological captivity of our war-making strategy that defeated us as other single factors. We thought it safer, cheaper, and cleaner to park our planes on Guam, fly at 37,000 feet, and bomb folks en masse.

There are those who say this is also the way to reach large cities. Huge media strategies, technological ministries, and program specialists—all purport to cover the tracks of local churches that flee to suburbs or nicer neighborhoods in the name of larger budgets for missions.[14]

Kenneth Scott Latourette has suggested that between AD 500-1500 the church did not grow. It exchanged real estate: Africa for Europe. One wonders if that isn't happening now in the exchange of cities for suburbs and small towns.

The systematic penetration by churches of neighborhoods, high-rise buildings, unions, factories, public schools, parks, arts, and city halls can no more be compensated for by temporal strategies in the United States than in India or Brazil. Why is it heroic for the missionary to live in a jungle but stupid, even presumptuous, to live in city neighborhoods with our families? Have we forgotten how many families we buried, how many of our children died or were badly educated in the pioneer rural mission of the church?[15]

The Challenge of Unreached Peoples

Most pastors and missionaries in any environment design ministry strategies they are comfortable with, in the same way that we ask our congregation to sing the songs we like. Most start with ourselves as the norm or given, then try to stretch toward those who are different with various degrees of success.

Perhaps we should, instead, make our starting point the unreached themselves. Then we can work back to the method, structure, and leadership style that will make it happen.

For example, a young man sat in a Chicago Loop restaurant watching the hundreds of young professionals flood in for lunch and thought about how one would reach them for Jesus Christ. By definition they were the urban wine-and-cheese crowd, twenty to thirty years old—mostly single or if married, childless—on a fast track of upward mobility in a profession. The young pastor reasoned rightly that the restaurant might be the best place to start the church, and the Sunday services strategy would need to be very different from the traditional church these multitudes refused to attend. He further reasoned that his own evangelistic and pastoral strategies and his priorities of programs needed to be very different from any of those traditional churches that do not reach young Loop professionals. Right again! It would be much harder to do, of course, usually because the mission leaders won't know how to promote and how to fund such urban church development philosophy and strategy. It is much easier to move into neighborhoods where churches already exist and function like competing fast-food hamburger chains. You assume it is more efficient to start where we already know a hamburger market exists, then get them to eat our "better" hamburgers.

Urban churches do this all over the globe. We do not go where no churches exist or to the truly unreached urban peoples. Instead, we go where other churches already are and market our product. There is some validity to this urban mission marketing strategy of course. Just don't call it urban evangelism or *new* church development.

The Barriers to Large City Evangelization

Since 1981 the Lausanne Committee for World Evangelization has implemented a series of almost sixty urban evangelism consultations in some of the world's largest cities on six continents. In cities as diverse as Cairo, Mexico City, Bombay, Belgrade, and Copenhagen, participants have been asked to identify the major barriers to evangelization. Curiously, responses generally fall into two basic categories.

1. Barriers in the church
2. Barriers in the city

More often than not, the consultants would find that on any list of ten barriers, at least half and usually more than half would be within the church or mission itself. In other words, the primary barriers to evangelization of our large cities are factors which the church can influence or change directly if it would.

Several formats have been used for these urban evangelism consultations. Briefly they include the following elements.

The Key Urban Leaders Evangelization Consultation

Four groups of leaders (key urban pastors of various denominations, mission decision makers, seminary professors or leadership developers, and lay professionals) come together for two or three days of study, prayer, sharing, and strategizing about ways that empower the whole church to take the whole gospel to the whole city.

The Urban Evangelism Models and Strategies Conference

The varieties of urban ministry programs and resource persons of many groups are presented in on-site visits or assessed in case study workshops, so these resources can be multiplied among other ministry designers. Participants may number up to 200 persons and are usually chosen by a denominationally diverse planning committee.

The Urban Evangelism Conference

This is an inspirational and informative lay event with plenary sessions and workshops on a range of personal evangelism issues and strategies. It is by invitation. From five hundred to one thousand participants attend.

The Regional City's Leaders Evangelization Consultation

On a large national or regional format, model and strategy resources are brokered for the church's total urban mission: worship, evangelism, discipleship, stewardship, fellowship, and service.

The Special Theme Urban Mission Conference

Here a single theme might be the fundamental organizing principle. These themes might be included.
The urban refugee
The elderly, youth, unemployed, and so forth
The chemically dependent unreached people
The lay professional in urban mission
The urban pastor
Media and communications
Mission and institutions: hospitals, schools, jails, and so forth

The gospel and the slum—or the high rise
The urban family

Meeting at Pattaya, Thailand, in 1980, urban church leaders from all six continents met to share resources and strategies for the evangelization of large cities. Over and over, while admitting that we evangelicals really do not know enough about large cities and are seriously threatened by their rapid growth and pervasive power, the major barriers or failures are primarily ecclesiastical and not environmental.[16]

Clearly the Lord is urbanizing his world and internationalizing his cities. He is bringing the whole world across oceans to large cities everywhere. So the urban mission hardly needs to cross oceans any more. It only needs to cross cultures to reach the world in the city.

Europe today presents "The Empire Strikes Back" syndrome. London used to be *caput munde* head of the world. Now the world lives in London. It may be the best place to evangelize Pakistanis, Arabs, or other groups. Amsterdam once ruled Surinam and Indonesia. Now those groups live near the canals in that city. Fourteen percent of Paris is Algerian. Hundreds of thousands from Turkey live in German cities. Some of the most creative and effective evangelism of Yugoslavs today is going on among the 50,000 guest workers commuting in Stockholm.

About one million Japanese live in Sao Paulo, Brazil. Obviously, some new partnerships are needed between the churches of Japan and Brazil. The Lausanne Chinese Committee has divided the whole world into thirty-eight Chinese regions for evangelism. It is a new day of opportunity. The foreign mission is coming home to every large city.

Surely now with our computers we can study and track these large cities and the peoples within them. We can also do our church census studies and gather the case studies that show who is reaching whom, where, and how. Then we can, indeed *must,* share this information in nonpaternalistic or triumphalistic ways with other church and mission groups who care about the evangelization of the whole city. Then we should develop urban ministry internships at least regionally for every major large city in the world.

There may be subsequent reasons to reshape the list, but eleven major urban regions suggest themselves for urban mission and evangelism strategies

1. North Asian Rim
2. ASEAN (Association of Southeast Asian Nations)
3. India
4. Africa West
5. Africa South and Central
6. Mediterranean
7. East Europe Block
8. North and West Europe
9. Hispanic (Miami to Buenos Aires)
10. Brazil
11. North America

There are no longer valid reasons to postpone concerted, collaborative urban mission strategies within the parameters of the Lausanne Covenant definition of evangelism for each of these major urban regions.

God help us to do it.

Notes

1. The Unreached Peoples concept is generally familiar now because of the mission annuals coming out of MARC, 919 West Huntington; Monrovia, CA 91016.
2. Elfan Rees, *We Strangers and Afraid.*
3. By count of the author.
4. Data-filled books on world cities appear regularly from Sage Publications in Beverly Hills, CA. In fact, they publish *Urban Affairs* annual reviews which are helpful. Also see books like *Six Billion People: Demographic Dilemmas and World Polities,* by George Tapinos and Phyllis T. Piotro (McGraw Hill: New York, 1978), The World Watch materials from Washington D.C., a new Cambridge series of urban volumes edited by West Africa's best known urbanologist, Kenneth Little.
5. Roy Hofheinz and Kent Calder, *Eastasia Edge* (Basic Books, 1982). This gives a dramatic description of the Asianization of the world.
6. Lewis Wirth. See the article "Cities" in the *Encyclopedia of the Social Sciences* by Lewis Mumford which discusses an interpretative essay on cities. Also see Mumford in his many books on cities and authors like Eames and Goode, *Anthropology*

of the City: An Introduction to Urban Anthropology (Englewood Cliffs: Prentice-Hall, 1977).

7. Rachelle B. Warren and Donald I. Warren, *The Neighborhood Organizer's Handbook* (South Bend: University of Notre Dame Press, 1977).

8. There are many standard texts for students of cities. My favorite is *The Urban World*, 2nd ed. by J. John Palen (McGraw Hill, 1981) because the section on urbanization in the lesser-developed world compares and contrasts American cities with those abroad in useful ways.

9. The best description of this "overload" phenomenon is in *Science,* June 1970.

10. Cairo will illustrate the point but inquires show it is not unique. There were thirty-three students in the Coptic Evangelical Seminary (Presbyterian) in May, 1983. Not one student came from the many churches of Cairo.

11. The documentation for these assertations can be found in *Latin American Urbanization* by Douglas Butterworth and K. Chance, (New York: Cambridge University Press, 1981), one of the superb volumes in the expanding Cambridge series, "Urbanization in Developing Countries."

12. I think that 95 percent of our effective urban evangelism is probably through these three sets of primary relationships. Our pastors should help members to make three charts to identify and strategize for evangelization within them. Usually this will be far more fruitful than door-to-door or other "cold contact" approaches.

13. I rather impertinently and routinely suggest that every mission agency headquarters draw a two mile circle around their urban building location and create a research and development component to test new models and train new personnel. Encouragement for my suggestion comes from essays like *Modern Organizations* by Amitai Etzioni (Englewood Cliffs: Prentice Hall, 1964).

14. The technologizing of our foreign and urban mission has many obvious benefits, and it will happen no matter what I think about it. But some of the side effects should be addressed such as the perpetual dependence of Third World or urban peoples upon outsiders who perpetuate information control of budgets, policies, and decision making.

15. The author has been confronted with these comments for twenty years.

16. See the Lausanne Occasional Paper, No. 9, "The Thailand Report," *Christian Witness to Large Cities,* edited by the author. Many Southern Baptists from different continents participated in these consultations and their work is part of the brief report.

5

Non-Christian Religion and Culture in the Cities of the World

M. Thomas Starkes

In the 1980s the non-Christian religions are on the march in such unusual places as London, Brussels, and San Diego. Major cities have become the backdrop for a syncretistic mix of mosques, gurus, and corner altars dedicated to objects of worship hitherto unknown in those locales. In London the elegant Regent's Park Mosque is one of the most beautiful worship centers built in England in the past quarter century. In nearby Brent, England, Muslims pray in what was once a Reformed Church building. In the east of London Muslims have bought an old synagogue and are now using it as a mosque. In Brussels one can see devout Muslims all over the city dropping to their knees and foreheads to observe their noon prayer ritual. In Stuttgart, Mercedes Benz has built a company mosque for its Turkish and European convert workers. The cities of France in 1984 contain more than two million Muslims. A new mosque was completed in 1980 in Rome where its call to prayer is within hearing of the Vatican itself.

San Diego reflects the North American cities flooded within the past decade with Oriental religions. Americanized gurus mix with Nichiren Buddhists and Arab Muslims on the busy streets and market places, each vying for new converts from the Catholic and Protestant Christians there. The largest world cities and their respective religious makeup are indicative of the task ahead for Christian missions and evangelism. Here are some examples.

1. Mexico City—Catholic/Christian
2. Tokyo—Secularist/Shinto
3. New York City—Christian/Jewish

4. Calcutta—Hindu
5. Peking—Communist
6. London—Christian/Secularist

These and other major world cities frame the backdrop for the battle for human allegiance.

Aggressive world religionists are changing the demographic environment in which the Christian mission task is being conducted. These aggressive persons present informed Christians renewed opportunities for dialogue, interaction, and evangelism.

Christianity today battles for human allegiance among four major competitors in world cities.

1. Hinduism—with 600 million adherents
2. Buddhism—with 500 million adherents
3. Islam—with 800 million adherents
4. Communism—with 1.5 billion adherents

These are treated in this chapter in the order of their chronological appearance on the world scene. The chapter concludes with suggested guidelines for Christian response to their presence and power.

Hinduism

Hinduism remains the major religion of India, the world's second most populous nation. Along with two of its offshoots, Jainism and Sikhism, Hinduism accounts for more than four fifths of the Indian subcontinent's people. But, more important for our consideration here, Hinduism and its adherents refuse to stay home. They have made their way into most of the major cities of the world, especially in the West. Therefore, Hinduism deserves treatment in this chapter on the changing cultural and religious makeup of the world's urban areas.

Basic Beliefs

Most Hindus hold that the nature of ultimate reality or impersonal absolute (Brahman) is ultimately unknowable by persons. Yet a person is seen as a part of Brahman who can realize union with this high god. In the realization of this oneness persons can achieve greatness through godhood. Vishnu is worshipped as one of the gods who becomes incarnate at will and is very popular with the masses because of this power of reincarnation. Siva is another of the hundreds of gods within Hinduism. He is seen as the creator-destroyer-sustainer of life. He is a popular god despite the fact that he supposedly promotes endurance of pain, starvation, and solitary meditation.

Karma is seen by Hindus as a law which states that every responsible decision must have its consequences. It is a principle of moral reaction applied to both good and evil actions. Bound up with Karma is the assumption of suwsara, or the rebirth or transmigration of the soul. What persons desire most is deliverance, or Moksa, from the endless cycle of reincarnation governed by Karma and the limitations of individual existence. So this life is not what each person is searching for. He or she desires, instead, escape from this life to a higher level of godlike existence. The message of Hinduism seems to be something like this: live out life doing what is known to be right so that finally entry may be made into eternal peace through deliverance from the limitations of this present deceptive life.

East/West Collision

Religions from the East have collided with those in the West with a resounding thud in the past decade and a half. The reverberation is still being heard today. American cities have felt the impact of such Hindu cults as Transcendental Meditation. More than a million US citizens in the past fifteen years have paid an average of $115 each for introductory courses in TM. Currently an average of almost a thousand persons are initiated into TM daily. The Student's International Meditation Society grossed more than 40 million dollars in 1983.

The official TM stance is that TM is not a religion. This is a highly questionable claim. It was introduced to the US in the late 1960s by Maharishi Mahesh Yogi, a guru trained and commissioned by another guru.

Another Hindu cult in the United States today is ISKCON, or the International Society for Krishna Consciousness. These Krishna chanters maintain that the Hindu god Krishna had 16,108 wives and

161,000 children. That is, Krishna first married eight queens. Later he married 16,100 princesses at the same moment by expanding himself into 16,100 forms and then had ten sons by each one. All these marriages, the Krishna devotees assert, were pure relationships and not flawed by lust or material yearnings.

The most recent reincarnation of Krishna was the Lord Caitanya who appeared almost five hundred years ago. Lord Jesus and Lord Buddha were also avatars or representatives of the Lord Krishna. Krishna, it is held, is supposed to return in about another five hundred years, this time riding a white horse and bearing the name Kalki.

ISKCON has a strong sense of group support and identity as they congregate and concentrate on major US cities. They are but part of the Hindu invasion into the Western world.

India/Bangladesh/Pakistan

Bangladesh is 86 percent Muslim and 13 percent Hindu. The other 1 percent is shared between Christians, Buddhists, and animists. Metropolitan Dacca has a population of almost 3 million and there are over 1 million in Chittagong. The population density of the country is 1,513 people per square mile in an area slightly smaller than Wisconsin. The population of Pakistan is 95 million. The people are 97 percent Muslim. The other 3 percent is almost equally divided between Christians and Hindus. Karachi has a population of almost 5 million and Lahore almost 3 million. Lyallpur has just over 1 million. The population density of the entire nation is 234 people per square mile in an area just larger than Texas.

India has a population of 730 million. The population density is 511 people per square mile in an area one third the size of the United States. The people are 83 percent Hindu, 11 percent Muslim, 3 percent Christian, and 2 percent Sikh. India has been independent since 1947 and became a democratic republic in 1950. More than 12 million Hindu and Muslim refugees crossed the India-Pakistan borders in the mass migration of 1948.

Calcutta has a population approaching 10 million. Greater Bombay has over 8 million and Madras has almost 6 million. Ahmadabad has almost 3 million and Bangalore has around 2.5 million. Other cities in India with over a million population are Kanpur (1.8); Poona (1.8); and Nagpur (1.4).

The combined populations of those nations on the Indian subcontinent is almost a billion. These nations, with their Hindu-Muslim mix, represent about 20 percent of the earth's population. Their cities cry out for effective and compassionate Christian ministry and witness.

Receptivity Reexamined

Word came from India in 1983 that more than 90,000 Christians had reconverted back to Hinduism during the previous year. The strong SSS movement was partly responsible for this phenomenon. It is a popular and militant attempt to remind residents of India that their cultural and religious loyalties belong with Hinduism. This is given impetus by Mrs. Gandhi's skepticism about the continued active role of evangelical missionaries and the resulting lack of visas for such purposes.

In spite of this movement, church growth in India remains active. For example, India is now second only to the United States in the number of Baptists. In the midst of religious upheaval on the Indian subcontinent, the challenge of Hinduism is one demanding nothing short of everything for the Christian urban strategist. Especially successful will be those efforts combining social ministry and verbal witness. This will partially meet the needs of the tremendous mass of humanity in India.

Buddhism

Two Major Types

Modern Buddhism is most clearly and commonly divided between two large schools, the Hinayana ("small raft") and the Mahayana ("large raft"). At times the Hinayana sect is called "The Way of the Elders" or Theravada. In order to remember the distinctives of the two groups, the reader may find this chart helpful:

Hinayana	Mahayana
Sutra	Shastra
Monk	Lay person
Sri Lanka, Burma	Korea, Japan, USA
Conservative	Liberal
Gautama Buddha	Bodhisattva
Thin Buddha	Fat Buddha
Individual	Community

In Hinayana, or Theravada, Buddhism, the ideal is the monk. The monk is seen as embodying self-denial and an individualistic approach in questing after Nirvana. This quest is to be guided by consulting only the Sutras or the original sayings of Buddha. The original Buddha remains the model and is pictured as thin and unsmiling. Hinayana Buddhism is also sometimes called Southern Buddhism and predominates in Sri Lanka, Burma, and Thailand.

Mahayanists regard the Shastras, or commentaries on the Sutras, as being almost on a par with the original sayings of Buddha. Both constitute sacred literature for them. Mahayanists do not emulate and idealize the monk but have respect for the Bodhisattva, a term referring to one who has attained his own salvation but voluntarily renounces it out of compassion for his fellow humans when he actively seeks to lead them to salvation even though it may require countless rebirths. Mahayana Buddhists stress community effort to achieve Nirvana. They are not nearly so individualistic as their counterparts, the Hinayanists.

However, it should be noted that the two major schools within Buddhism do hold certain truths in common in spite of their vast differences. These truths include: (1) moderation as a way of life; (2) overcoming evil with good and love; (3) anger, envy, and jealousy are the roots of evil; (4) the undoing of ego through wisdom; and (5) life as everfleeting or disappearing.

Western Intrusion

Chinese Mahayana Buddhism reached Japan five centuries after Christ, having come through Korea. In the past score of years, Mahayana Buddhism came from Japan to the United States. The major divisions in the United States follow the three major sects of Mahayana Buddhism found in Japan: (1) the "Pure Land" sects, (2) the "intuitive" or meditative sects as in Zen, and (3) the "sociopolitical" symbolized by Soka Gakkai.

The "Pure Land" sects in the United States have taken the form of the Buddhist Churches of America. This organization presently publishes a series of tracts, a newsletter, and a monthly leaflet entitled "The American Buddhist." In some respects these American Buddhists are much like American Protestants. For example, there is a strong educational and social emphasis because the organization teaches that it is not necessary to withdraw from the world to become a perfect Buddhist. To survive, its adherents must continue to struggle with the question of relating a basically Japanese religion to American culture.

The most militant and flourishing company of Buddhists in the United States is the Nichiren Sho-shu Association or as it is known in Japan, Sokagakkai. This religious group now numbers more than 16 million in Japan and has 250,000 members in the US. Sokagakkai is one of the more than 350 of the "new religions" in Japan. In 1946, when the U. S. Army and political rulers arrived in postwar Japan, a state of martial law was declared and the emperor was forced to deny that he was divine. The state religion of Shinto was declared officially nonexistent. As the people of Japan found themselves in a religious identity crisis, almost overnight the "new religions" sprang up giving new forms of religious expression. Elements of Shinto reappeared under new forms. Sokagakkai practitioners give twice daily chants of Nam Myoho Renge Kyo ("Hail to the Wonderful Law of the Lotus Sutra"). In return for this faithful chanting, Sokagakkai promises physical healing, personal fortune, and protection from accidents.

In 1965 Sokagakkai began to make serious inroads into the American scene where it is usually known as the Nichiren Sho-shu Association or NSA. That same year saw the establishment of the American newspaper entitled *The World Tribune.* The newspaper regularly features photos of happy pilgrims who have been to Japan to soak up the miracles of the headwaters at the chief Sokagakkai shrine.

Sokagakkai, under the name of the Nichiren Sho-shu Association, has a bright future in the United States as it gains roots in native Americana. It will continue to appeal to those who seek instant material blessings for chanting the required chant.

Zen is by far the most popular form of Buddhism in the United States. Its practice often cuts across lines of religious preference. Zen has been in the United States officially since 1930 when the Zen Institute in America was founded.

Zen is almost impossible to define because it shuns the expression of reality in any ideas or concepts. Zen insists that ultimate truth can only be known intuitively. Zen is usually presented as spontaneity. However, historically, there are direct ties between Zen and classic Buddhism. Therefore, Zen may be defined as "That school of enlightenment born from the mystical stream in Buddhism."

The greatest interpreter of Zen to the Western world in the twentieth century has been D. T. Suzuki, author of *A Manual of Zen Buddhism*. Suzuki's primary strength was his ability to phrase Zen in concepts readily understandable to interested Americans. Here are three examples.

1. The foundation of all concepts is simple, unsophisticated experience.
2. The ordinary logical process of reasoning is powerless to give final satisfaction to our deepest needs.
3. To be free, life must be an absolute affirmation.[1]

Zen can be an instantaneous awareness caused by a perplexing conversation with a teacher. Zen may also be abandoning all efforts for self-fulfillment as in this poem.

> When one looks at it,
> One cannot see it.
> When one listens for it,
> One cannot hear it.
> But when one uses it,
> It is inexhaustible.

Or Zen may be a living awareness of all of life being a part of one reality. Zen may be ceasing to struggle over one of the 1700 classic

Zen Koans or riddles. Zen is wherever persons are seeking enlightenment through meditation or looking for oneness with reality.

It is clear that the Eastern-based religion called Buddhism is in the midst of a clearly documented Western intrusion. Zen, Sokagakkai, and the Buddhist Churches of America are found in such cities as Honolulu, Chicago, and San Francisco as well as in Bangkok, Tokyo, and Seoul.

Self-Esteem and the Savior Among "Saviors"

The primary contribution of traditional (Hinayana) Buddhism to the world religion scene is that of *anatta* or "no soul." Meanwhile, one of the benefits of Christian discipleship is self-realization. Self-esteem is one of the fallouts of hearing and heeding Jesus' words, "I came that they may have life, and have it abundantly" (John 10:10). This fulfilled quest for individualistic salvation is bound to cause confrontations between those realizing their potential and Buddhist monks negating the ego. Hopefully, the dialogue between the two will afford evangelistic opportunities for Christians seeking to communicate the joy of the Spirit's fruit.

Islam

Islam is Christianity's major competitor in the world cities. There are now about 800 million Muslims in the world and about 1.2 billion followers of Christ. With such large numbers it is incumbent upon Christian urban mission strategists to plan a dialogue/evangelism model involving Muslims.

Muhammad: One Prophet

The prophet Muhammad was born about AD 570 in the city of Mecca. That urban center was a beehive of religious activity. It was located on the west coast of Arabia and lay on vital caravan routes. Muhammad was born into a clan which controlled the Kaaba stone. It was surrounded by relics, images, and paintings representative of numerous gods.

Marriage in a wealthy family afforded Muhammad the privilege of spending his days in meditation and solitude searching for the one true God. After almost fifteen years of such activity, Muhammad reported that the angel Gabriel appeared to him and called him to be the prophet of Allah, the one true God. As the prophet of Allah, Muhammad began to preach his new message revolving around the oneness of Allah to the citizens of Mecca.

In AD 630 with a force of ten thousand men, Muhammad captured the city and destroyed the images and idols at the Kaaba stone. Muhammad died in AD 632, the victim of poor health. The movement had been started with great force by this remarkable prophet.

Five Pillars

The serious Muslim practices his religious faith by means of the five "pillars" of Islam, so-called because they provide the practical support system of the Islamic faith.

Recitation of the creed. Once in his lifetime every Muslim must repeat with sincerity a creed, "There is no God but Allah and Muhammad is his prophet." Many devout Muslims repeat this creed numerous times each day. It is by the recitation of this creed that a Muslim is a Muslim.

Daily prayer. The faithful Muslim prays five times daily: at dawn, noon, mid-afternoon, at sunset, and before retiring. When praying, the Muslim is to look toward Mecca, the holy city.

Giving of alms. Each Muslim is to give one fortieth of his income and holdings to aid the poor. In actual practice, however, rich persons pay a higher percentage than do the poor. Those who are to receive this offering include slaves buying their freedom and strangers and wayfarers.

Fasting during Ramadan. The month of Ramadan in the fall commemorates the month when the Koran was received. This thirty-day period of fasting is concluded with a thirty-day feast.

Pilgrimage to Mecca. Once during his lifetime, every physically and financially able adult male Muslim is to take a trip to Mecca. Almost 200,000 pilgrims do so annually. During their stay in Mecca, the pilgrims must visit the well of Hagar and Ishmael. They must also walk seven times around the Kaaba and then kiss it. When the pilgrim returns home he may have the title "Hajji" attached to his name to show his peers that he has fulfilled this religious obligation. These five pillars or practices help to unite the Muslim world around the globe.

Major Beliefs

There are five basic beliefs to go with the five major practices of Islam, all based on the Koran.

The unity of Allah. Muhammad and his followers have for centuries stressed the fact of the divine in one God. There is no other God, period. Oddly enough, Muhammad urged the acceptance of Jesus as a prophet and even accepted the teaching concerning the virgin birth but denied strongly that Jesus was God.

Angels. Although Muslims profess to believe in one God, they give much attention to belief in angels. Gabriel is viewed as the supreme angel because he gave the Koran to Muhammad. Satan is considered as one of the angels as are the various *jinn,* from which comes the modern English word "genie."

The Prophets. Muslims believe that Allah has sent 124,000 prophets to mankind. Six of these are selected as the most important: Adam, Noah, Abraham, Moses, Jesus, and Muhammad. Muhammad is considered the "seal" of all the prophets, superior in both the temporal and qualitative sense.

The will of Allah. The Koran makes it clear that each person is to choose and follow freely the will of Allah. People are completely responsible for the choices they make. Allah, in his wisdom and mercy, allows persons to make choices in those moral areas in which they will be judged.

The day of judgment. Depending on how each person fares on the day of judgment, he or she will be sent to hell or heaven. The Muslim lives in dread of this day because he knows that Allah keeps an account of wrongs and rights and judges each person on that basis.

Key Divisions

Three sects within Islam are important for study here because of their influence in world cities outside traditional Arab territory.

First, Sufism (from an Arabic word *Sufi* which means "wool") refers to those Muslims who are interested in a direct, personal, and mystic experience with Allah. The Sufis have been very missionary and have taken their brand of the Islamic faith to India, most nations of Africa, Indonesia, and the United States. In turn, the Muslim Sufis have been influenced by Hindu and Christian mystics. The Sufis affirm that although persons are not God, they can be one mystically with Allah. Because a person can experience God directly, he or she does not need outside help from books or traditions.

A second sect within Islam is the Shiite, predominating in Iran. This group constitutes only about one twelfth of the total number of Muslims in the world. The Shiites are bound together by the belief that Ali, the son-in-law of Muhammad's true successor, is alive today speaking for all true Muslims.

Five out of six of all Muslims in today's world are called Sunnis. These are the orthodox within Islam. This group predominates in such nations as Saudi Arabia and Egypt.

Missions: Here and There

Most Westerners are amazed when they discover the remarkable growth of Islam into non-Arabic areas. In fact, the top five nations in the world in terms of number of Muslim adherents are non-Arabic. They are: Indonesia, India, Pakistan, Bangladesh, and the Soviet Union. It is becoming apparent that parts of western Europe are being rapidly Muslimized. For example, Muslims are advancing in such cities as London, Brussels, Paris, and Rome. This movement is even further compounded by the growth of Islam in the United States. There is a large training center in northern New Mexico turning out Muslim evangelists especially equipped to spread Islam among Americans. The more than five million Muslims in the U.S. in 1984 will probably grow to the point that there will be more Muslims than Jews by 1990.

Black Muslims: Radical Change

The Black Muslims (their name prior to 1975) today claim more than one million followers in the United States. With the conversion of the former Cassius Clay in 1965, the Lost Nation of Islam received international publicity.

A major change in the Black Muslims came in 1975 with the death of Elijah Muhammad. With the takeover of the movement by Wallace Deen Muhammad, the founder's son, the name of the movement became the World Community of Al-Islam in the West and in 1980 was changed again to the American Muslim Mission. Members can now salute the American flag, engage in politics, and serve as members of the armed forces. Wallace Deen Muhammad has said on numerous occasions, "Our purpose is the restoration of pure Islam." He has opened membership in the group to all races.

There is no religious group in American history that has shown such a radical change in its teaching and practice in the past decade than has the American Muslim Mission. The challenge of this formerly militant group has taken on a new form in such cities as Detroit and New Orleans. The challenge is now to meet the American Muslims in much the same manner as Christians might in Mecca or Beirut.

The Cross and the Sword Meet

The world urban centers are becoming the battleground for the allegiance of persons caught in the cross fire between Muslims and Christians. Beirut is the symbol of a militaristic confrontation between these two major faiths. In other areas the friction is not so abrasive, but the conflict rages. The cross and the sword have met and the outcome is dependent on the softening of these tools and the beginning of compassionate dialogue.

The growth of Islam is intensifying the conflict. This is so much the case that the lead article in April 1983, issue of Bulletin of the Council on the Study of Religion was entitled "Teaching Contemporary Islam." In that article the author John L. Esposito made this point.

Islamic studies has undergone a significant change in recent years. The Arab oil embargo and manifestation of Islamic revivalism have sparked new interest in Islam and in the Muslim. In particular, the political manifestations of a resurgent Islam with its geo-political significance has opened up a broad range of new opportunities and possibilities in teaching, publishing and consulting.

Wherever the cross and the sword meet, there are helpful and needed guidelines for dialogue.

One of the best guidelines for the witnessing and relating Christian is to become familiar with the Koran's presentation of Jesus. Jesus is pictured in the Koran as bringing the gospel as fulfillment of the Torah, showing the signs of Allah, teaching prayer, and being a prophetic witness to the existence of Allah. According to the Koran those who follow Jesus have a special covenant with Allah, and he will reward them on the day of the final resurrection and judgment.

The informed Christian who desires to relate to his Muslim friends should remember that Jesus' name is found ninety-seven times in the Koran. A good witnessing technique is to begin with the Koran's teaching about Jesus as virgin born, miracle worker, teacher, prophet, and the word of Allah. This can lead to an opportunity to present the fulfillment of God's will in the risen Lord.

The articulate Christian witness may have to deal also with the fact that some Muslims have a gross misconception about the Christian understanding of the Trinity. Some Muslims conceive of the Trinity as the Father, the Son, and the Virgin Mary. This misinformation must be corrected in the minds of Muslims to whom Christians are witnessing. One proven way to do this is to present God as one reality in three relationships.

More Keys to Christian Witness

For effective evangelism among Muslims in the world's major cities, there are more proven hints. These include: (1) The Muslim is commanded to read the Injil (Gospel) in the Koran, chapter 57, verse 27. (2) Jesus is presented as a servant in the Koran, chapter 19, verse 30. Reference can be made to the Suffering Servant passages in Isaiah. (3) The Muslim must be persuaded that the Christian faith is for all of life. He sometimes hears the gospel as relating only to the religious aspects of life. A partial gospel will not do.

Communism: Ideology or Idol?

More than one-fourth of all the citizens on planet earth in 1984 live under Communist domination. The Communist Party, by and large, determines for these 1.5 billion persons their life-styles, ideology, and fundamental behavior. Therefore, it is imperative for the urban missions strategists of the future to be informed about those areas dominated by this religiopolitical philosophy.

History: Marx and the Rise of Communism

Karl Marx was the son of a Jewish lawyer converted to the Christian faith when young Karl was but six years old. As a young student, Karl Marx was interested in becoming a professor. When he could not find a job teaching, he got a job as a reporter on a radical newspaper in Cologne. In 1845 Marx moved to Paris where he became editor of the *Franco-German Yearbook*. It was there he met Frederich Engels. Karl Marx moved to London in the late 1840s and in 1848 he wrote *The Communist Manifesto*. In 1867 Marx wrote *Das Kapital*, which has become the "Bible" of modern Communism.

Marx attacked Christianity on two counts. First, he felt it supports the affluent way of life. It gives support to the status quo for the masses who are taught to remain content in their poverty so they can be rewarded in heaven much later. Second, he believed Christians are deceived because they are told that there is a beyond. There is no beyond according to Marx. The only reality is matter in motion. He asserted that only by abandoning Christianity with its otherworldly hopes can persons be really happy.

Marx led none of the revolutions which puported to change his theory into political and economic reality. The first such revolution came in an unlikely place—Russia—through the efforts of Nicolai Lenin and his Bolsheviks. For Marx the liberation of the working class from the ruling capitalists was the task of the working class itself. But Russia largely lacked these capitalists and the factory workers who were to lead the revolution. Lenin instead called for a group of middle-class intellectuals who could inspire the masses with a spark of revolution. Lenin thus argued for a temporary rule

of the intelligentsia to wipe out the last vestiges of exploitation by
the Czar and the few capitalists. Lenin died in 1924. It was he who
helped Marx's "inevitable" revolution to come to fruition.

History: Since 1917

The history of Communism since the "October Revolution" in
Russia has been one of geographical expansion. By far the most
populous nation to come under Communist rule since 1917 has been
China.

The Chinese Communist Party was formed in Shanghai in 1921.
The years 1945-49 are designated by Chinese Communist historians
as the "Third Revolutionary Civil War." In 1949 the nationalistic
forces of Chiang Kai-shek were driven to Tawain. On October 1 the
Communist leaders proclaimed the existence of the People's Republic of China.

Today Chinese Communism is a unique entity with certain characteristics of its own. They have included:
1. large dependence on the training of the peasant masses;
2. "people's communes" in which up to five thousand families
   are joined together for production purposes;
3. spasmodic purges in which those who differ radically from
   Chinese Communist leadership are eliminated.

By the year 2000 Shanghai and Peking will be two of the ten
largest cities in the world. The population of China went past the one
billion mark early in 1983. This means that the masses living on
mainland China constitute about 22 percent of the total earth's population. There are some good reports on the progress of Christianity
in China but mainly among the rural masses. The cities of China are
relatively untouched.

There are few continents on the earth today not affected by Communism. Nicaragua and Cuba dot the Central American and Caribbean maps with red. Eastern European satellites of the Soviet Union
deny religious freedoms to Christians. Angola has become known as
a satellite of Russia through Cuban control. Afghanistan remains in
turmoil after the Russian army invasion late in 1981. Communist

history is thus one of continued military takeovers to aid the "inevitable" international revolution.

Basic Beliefs: A Religion?

Is Communism a religion? The answer must be in the affirmative. Communism has at least these four trappings of a religion: a founder; an eschatology; a value system; and an ethic.

The basic beliefs of Communism include the following:

1. economic motives and processes are always dominant;
2. human history is in a constant state of flux;
3. the true value of any commodity should be measured by the amount of labor used to produce it;
4. there is no God and religion is the "opiate of the people";
5. the end of all human effort will be a utopian society;
6. man has the capacity to build that utopian society without any help from a higher power.

Communism is a religion without a god as is classic Buddhism and Confucianism. It deserves to be ranked with major world religions.

Early Dialogue Attempts

Intense dialogue has been taking place for a score of years in Europe and Latin America. The results have been phenomenal on both sides of the conversation. Communists have admitted the naiveté of their view of man; that is, that he is able to lift himself out of his own squalor by the use of man-made forces and techniques. In turn, Christians have been forced to admit that by tradition they have fostered allegiance to an often-corrupt ruling class. Christianity is being correctly seen in the light of the realization that it cannot be concerned exclusively with the private faith of the individual but also with the building of a justice-oriented society.

These early Christian-Communist dialogues have produced outstanding Christian spokesmen for a theology of hope. One of these is Jurgen Moltman of the University of Tübingen. Dr. Moltman is critical of Communism's perversions such as the anticipation that "human emancipation of man will come automatically when the economic liberation of men in the socialist industrial state has taken place."[2]

This successful dialogue is proof that both Communists and Christians can converse and even change. When representatives of peoples numbering almost three billion converse, the world listens. There is more hope in constant dialogue than in suspicious hatred.

Liberation Theology: An Answer or a Clue?

Gustavo Gutierrez, a Catholic priest working in Latin America, wrote *A Theology of Liberation* in 1973. For most liberation theologians who have written since, Marxism is seen to provide the best possible understanding of suffering and oppression. This stance is often criticized by evangelical scholars who see liberation theology as being too heavily tied to a single view of the appropriate social order. Marxism is pictured by the critics as being inadequate because it does not take evil (sin) seriously enough. Therefore, Marxism can never be identified with the kingdom of God. The critics also contend that liberation theology, when it is related to Marxism, is too anthropocentric and secularistic.

On the other hand, some evangelical theologians are stressing the benefits of liberation theology. They maintain that this new movement is valuable because it warns of the dangers of civil religion, gives fresh perspectives on social ministries, calls attention to justice for the oppressed as a partner to salvation for the lost, and gives needed emphasis to seeing Christianity as ministering within its social context.

La Paz and Guatemala City join other Latin American cities as the backdrop for the struggle over liberation theology. At this stage, a decade after the movement became well-known, the jury is still out. However, it is seen by most evangelicals as having some value but tied too closely to Marxism. It is an attempt, at least, to mesh the gospel with social change.

A Christian Response

The religious allegiance of an individual or social group helps determine their cultural context and probably their response to the gospel. Therefore, the assumption that there is a "universal" way of communicating the gospel easily transferable to all cultures is false. Each cultural-religious context must be approached differently, bearing in mind the dominant religion of the area. At least four concerns are central to future mission effort in non-Christian contexts.

Information Gathering

The gathering of accurate information about non-Christian religions in world-class cities is indispensable for future mission strategy. This will avoid inaccurate stereotyping as well as providing possible "points of contact" for better communication. It is easier to dismiss the faiths and feelings of others as devilish, ignorant, or antisocial than it is to try to understand their religion and culture. It is also easier to view the insights of other religions as satanic. But the easy way out short-circuits both dialogue and evangelism.

Accurate information gathering involves more than a listing and comparison of doctrines. It also includes the collecting of data and impressions about myths, ethics, rituals, social mores, and experiences. The first three can be woven together to provide a framework for a set of beliefs. The last three center on common practices. Together all six go together to form a world view. The total world view must be considered in framing a mission strategy.

Analysis

The mere gathering of data pertinent to the dominant world view of a city is not sufficient. It is also incumbent upon mission strategists to analyze that data. At least five questions should be asked.

1. Is there a central point of contact that can be used by Christians in evangelism; for example, the rather high view of Jesus found in the Koran?
2. Is there a centrality in the world view for a certain type of moral behavior, that is, is there a form of Christian life-style that would be most attractive to the religious city dwellers in that context?
3. Which portions of the Bible will be most applicable to those

city dwellers with the dominant world view; for example the sacrifice by the priest among some animists?

4. Which aspects of the life of Jesus of Nazareth will have immediate appeal to members of the dominant group; for example, Jesus' teaching skills to those influenced by Confucianism?

5. Which elements of the dominant religion will be most likely to be responsive to the gospel *now;* for example, Jewish university students in Rio de Janeiro?

Rules for Dialogue

Open communication between witnessing Christians and non-Christians is far superior to stereotyped categorizing. There are some rules for interreligious dialogue on all levels. These rules include: (1) beginning with a stance of servanthood; (2) remembering that systems never meet but that persons do; (3) setting no limits on possible topics; (4) comparing the participants with their respective images of God, and not with the weaknesses of each other; (5) restating another's position to his satisfaction but reserving the right to disagree; and (6) continuing the process on an informal and experiential basis.

These proven guidelines can be valuable in increasing understanding and witnessing opportunities for Christians as they seek communication across cultural and religious lines.

Aggressive/Effective Evangelism

The hidden peoples of the world are increasing in urban areas as the non-Christian religions expand. To afford the majority of these persons the opportunity to receive Christ, there is no substitute for aggressive but effective evangelism. The evangelism of the future, which takes into consideration differing world views, must have at least four qualities:

1. It must be truly and totally biblical. "Soul-winning;" that is, a partial witness to a segment of each individual person is doomed to failure. This is because world views formed by

Communism, Hinduism, Buddhism, and Islam call for commitment to all portions of life.

2. It must be experimental and creative. To discover a pocket of persons who are Muslim, for example, is just the beginning of the task. New techniques such as mosque-church exchanges must be tried.

3. It must be based on priority. "Church as usual" will not do the job in the US or abroad. This means, simply stated, that certain activities now done will have to be dropped and others, such as neighborhoods targeted for ministry, must be begun.

4. It must be optimistic. At times the task seems overwhelming. So is God's love when presented by creative and compassionate Christians.

Conclusion

Cities change constantly. The gospel remains constant. The friction between these two truths cannot be ignored. This dilemma must be met with enlightened compassion. The challenge of the world cities is there in the form of non-Christian world views. The perspective of the gospel's side is one of optimism. The Savior's love is worthy of the task. Let those who love him show his love to the urbanites of our earth.

Notes

1. D. T. Suzuki, *An Introduction to Zen Buddhism.* (New York: Grove Press, Inc., 1964), p. 1.
2. *Openings for Marxist-Christian Dialogue,* Thomas W. Ogletree, ed. (Nashville: Abingdon Press, 1969).

6

Urban Ministry in Third World Cities: Three Examples

Jimmy Maroney   Ronald Hill   David Finnell

The huge urban population of the developing world can provoke either excitement for Christians in America as we consider the many opportunities for witness and the openness to the gospel in thousands of cities, or it can provoke depression if we dwell on the immensity of the task. The task is no doubt a giant one, and our missionary force may seem puny in light of the millions without Christ in the cities. Yet we are called to go, and as we go we remember that the harvest is not ours: it belongs to Christ.

In this chapter we highlight the work of three men for whom the cities have been an exciting and effective place of ministry. Not that what they have done has been easy—it has not. But they illustrate what can be done by men and women who are called, who have a heart for the city, and who have the skills to do the difficult work of urban ministry. First we observe the work of Jimmy Maroney as he sought to understand the city and people of Nairobi, Kenya, in East Africa and to move from this understanding to the development of new African churches—led by Kenyans. Second, we travel to Bangkok, Thailand, as Ronald Hill describes the systematic method that his mission and Thai Christians used to create new strategies for evangelism. Finally, in the third section David Finnell demonstrates how the Baptist Centre for Urban Studies was able to revitalize efforts to reach Singapore for Christ (the editors).

Nairobi

Despite its predominantly rural character, Africa is experiencing rapid urban growth. Spurred by high rates of natural increase (3.0

percent) and rural-urban migration, cities and towns in all African countries are expanding in population, settled area, and complexity. In less than a generation, towns which were previously small colonial capitals have become cities of over one million persons while rural villages have become regional marketing centers.

Although only about 27 percent of its population was classified as "urban" in 1983, Africa has a growing "urban problem" with an urban population of about 139 million out of a total African population of 513 million. The urban population is expected to grow to over 345 million by the year 2000. This projected increase represents the creation of about 66 cities the size of Lagos or 129 new centers the size of Nairobi. The size of the urban population represents an important new addition to the African landscape during the next sixteen years.

Demographic evidence indicates that about 30 percent of the continental urban population is concentrated in large cities, usually the capitals. A sample of thirty-five capital cities shows they are growing at about 8.5 percent annually compared to average national urban rates of about 6 percent and national population growth rates of 2.9 percent. Analysts believed that such growth rates were statistical anomalies a few years ago, that is, high growth rates on low bases, and there is evidence that rates have declined somewhat as bases have grown. It is nevertheless ensured that existing large cities will become much larger, and substantial growth will also occur in secondary urban centers.

Nairobi is the capital of the east African country of Kenya. The country's population in 1975 was 13.5 million, with 11.8 percent urban population. In 1980 there were 16.5 million Kenyans with an urban population of 13.5 percent. By the year 2000 Kenya will have over 37 million people with an urban population of 21.9 percent. Kenya in 1983 had the highest birth rate in the world with the average Kenyan woman having eight children.

Christianity was first introduced to Kenya in 1498 by men sailing with Vasco de Gama. The ship stopped in the bay of what is now Malindi. David Barrett says, "African response to Christianity was instantaneous and immense from the earliest days."[1] Christian growth continues in modern Kenya and today over eleven million in Kenya claim to be Christian in some fashion. Baptist churches have shared in this growth, which is not limited to Kenya. In eastern and southern Africa, Baptists are growing an estimated fourteen times faster than the population. Other Christian groups have been growing at a similar rate. Dr. Barrett has predicted that practically all East Africa will be Christian at the end of this century.

Nairobi, City in the Sun, is located 5600 feet above sea level in the central province of Kenya. It is a modern city that prides itself in being the unofficial capitol of Black Africa and the headquarters of many Third World organizations. It is a relatively young city having only been incorporated as a municipality in 1927. The present population is 1.6 million, but demographers are predicting a city population of 4.9 million in the year 2000.

The city's economic story can be told in brief: chronic unemployment, large labor force without skills, inadequate housing, and constant shortages of raw materials. The political condition up to August 1982 was stable. Since then, the country has been tense. The August abortive coup has left some unresolved questions and the life of the country has not returned to normal. Perhaps an era ended and a new one began that hot August night. Still, the church is growing in Kenya.

I began work in Nairobi in April of 1979. The first thing I did was to make a survey of the entire city. Notes from a diary dated June 1, 1979, revealed the following:

Languages: 70 vernacular languages, dominant languages are
Swahili, Kikuyu, and English
Christian Churches: 371
Muslim: 18
Hindu: 12
Jain: 12
Sikh: 8
Jehovah's Witness: 8

During the months of June, July, and August, I began to interview people who had been involved with mass evangelism in Nairobi. Men such as Billy Graham, Oral Roberts, and Tom Osborne had all held large rallies in Nairobi in the past ten years. Conferences such as Keswich, Annual Student Christian Fellowship, World Vision Pastor's Conference, and various charismatic meetings were held in the city during the past fifteen years.

The most recent mass evangelistic effort was conducted by Campus Crusade in 1978. Nairobi became the first African city to use the American import called "I Found It." The purpose of the campaign was to raise up a trained army within the church to evangelize Nairobi. It was hoped that through a media blitz, non-Christians would be put in touch with trained Christians.

"I Found It" was a pilot project and has since been used in various African cities. The plan was simple. After a heavy mass media campaign, interested people were asked to go to a "drop box" or "information center" where a trained person would deal with their spiritual needs.

There were 2,500 people trained in personal evangelism and about 15,000 people made recorded decisions. Follow-up on new Christians was left to the participating churches. *Lessons for New Christians* from Campus Crusade could be used if churches so desired.

Media cost was nearly $65,000.

In interviews with national Christian leaders who participated in "I Found It," the main problem with the project appeared to be cultural. For example, it was suggested that the slogan "I Found It" was an incomplete thought and therefore could have been better stated in a phrase like "I Found New Life in Jesus." Other suggestions were that more prayer before and after the campaign should have been scheduled; there should have been more emphasis put on the local church, and mass evangelism is not the best method which could have been employed.

Personally, I felt if the city had been divided into ten areas or districts, the plan would have been more effective. Attempting to deal with a city of one million proved to be too much to handle.

In late September 1979 I began to read the *Nairobi Metropolitan Growth Strategy,* a three-volume study produced by the Nairobi Urban Study Group and the World Bank in 1973. In Volume 2, I discovered the map (p. 122) that showed the direction the city would grow. It opened my eyes to a simple fact. The city can only grow in one direction—to the northeast. Because the city is bounded by a game park on the south, good farming land to the west, and a protected forest on the north, only the northeast is available for new housing development.

One key element of our strategy for Nairobi was the training of the laity. The explosion of Pentecostalism in Latin America convinced me that we had to focus on the laity if we hoped to grow in Nairobi. The greatest untapped resource of Christ is church members who have never been adequately discipled, who have not yet been trained or challenged to become bearers of the good news to their neighborhoods. Therefore, in the evenings during the months of November-December 1979 and January-March 1980, I went to every Baptist church in the Nairobi Baptist Association and taught evangelism, discipleship, and various models that could be used in an urban setting. I found the best way to design an urban strategy was to involve the ones who will implement it. Baptist church members were the key to evangelizing Nairobi. I was simply a resource person to pastors and church members. It was my job to motivate, enable, and become a catalyst during the next two years.

Another element in our strategy was understanding the northeast section of Nairobi. If this were the section of the city that was having the most rapid growth numerically, then we must understand the area. We learned the area could be viewed as layers of people. Not everyone can be viewed on the same level; layers or groups can be distinguished by age, education, language, sex, wealth, origin, and the way they live by neighborhoods.

Looking at the map of Nairobi, you can identify the following housing areas: Buru Buru, Umoja, Doonholm, Dandora, and Kariobangi, all on the Outer Ring Road of Nairobi. I personally spent time in these areas in order to develop a firsthand knowledge of the people and the geographical layout of this vast area. Walking or riding a bicycle proved to be a great way to do an in-depth study of a large area. It took me about three months before I felt that I knew the neighborhoods. Some were completed areas, and some were in

Figure 3
DISTRIBUTION OF POPULATION IN NAIROBI: 2000 AD

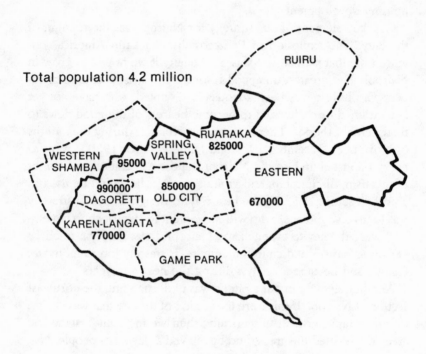

Source: *Nairobi Metropolitan Growth Strategy*, Vol. 2 (Nairobi, Kenya: Nairobi Urban Study Group, 1983).

the process of being completed. Others had people living in houses on one side of the street and work crews on the other side. Let me briefly describe each neighborhood or estate area.

Buru Buru is made up of two and three bedroom condo-type houses. They are all white with orange clay roofs. Rent is about $250-$350 per month. Buru Buru has its own schools, community center, and shopping center. Residents earn about $500 per month. Most have cars, and practically all the wives work. The population is 67,000.

Umoja is middle class with individual or detached houses that are very small and spaced close together. The units rent for about $180 per month. Only about 30 percent of the residents have cars. Fewer of the wives work. The population is 43,500.

Dandora is a low middle-class area with the people building their own houses with loans from the government. Residents earn about $100 per month. The population is 56,500.

Doonholm is a middle-class area with two and three bedroom houses of approximately 1000 square feet. Houses sell for about $27,500. Residents earn about $250-$400 per month. Cars are plentiful and the wife usually works. The average age is between 26-39 years of age. The population in 1980 was 21,000, but by 1985 it will mushroom to 61,000.

Kariobangi is an older neighborhood with people earning anywhere from $50-$100 per month. The houses are four units to a block. The Kariobangi Baptist Church was started in a house and is presently averaging 300-450 in worship services. The population is 87,000.

The combined population of these areas was conservatively estimated at 275,000 people in 1980. By 1985, 550,000 people will be occupying houses that are now being built.

Each of the five estate areas varies in its responsiveness. For example, the low economic area of Dandora is very responsive while Buru Buru is more secular minded and reserved. It was decided that we should attempt to plant a new church in these four estate areas: Buru Buru, Umoja, Dandora, and Doonholm.

The question of *how* a church was to be planted came immediately

Figure 4
MAP OF NAIROBI, KENYA

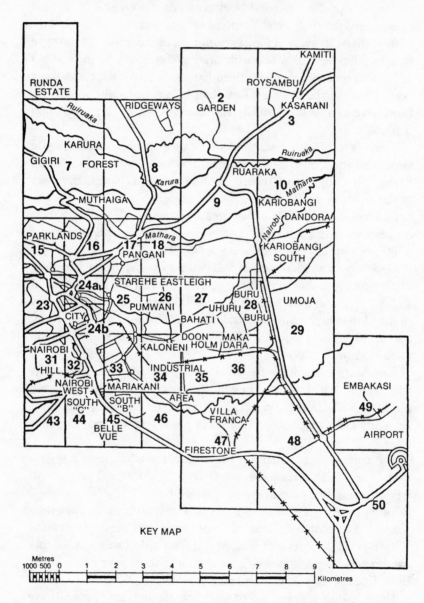

KEY MAP

to mind. What methods would we use? Was there a model for urban church planting that we could adapt? What resources would we need? Which estate area would we use as the pilot for the other three? These questions and many more were raised.

First, we discovered the fact that the Holy Spirit was already at work in Doonholm. A police supervisor volunteered his house to be used as a house church. Second, we found that house visitation was still the best way to publicize the Sunday morning service at House Number 120 in Doonholm. To establish our presence in the community, we had to show we were willing to meet their needs; therefore, we did a lot of things like providing transportation back home when a family member died, and we gave some food when one man lost his job.

Within six months, the house church in Doonholm taught me four things: (1) Bible teaching must be the primary act in worship, (2) good music is a necessity, (3) expect good stewardship from the people at the very beginning, and (4) a good organization keeps a house church operating. More will be said about house churches later.

We developed different approaches for each area we attempted to penetrate. There is no *one* way to do urban evangelism. Consequently, each area had to be approached differently. It is a comforting thought that the Holy Spirit will guide us when we attempt to evangelize any area!

We began work in Dandora in a rather unusual way. The area is very densely populated and there were few choices where a group could meet. The houses were small. Land was at a premium. It was rainy season and we could not meet outside. Finally, we located a large community-type building the Presbyterian Church administrated. We contacted the administrator and spoke with him about holding Sunday worship services in the building. The only time he would give us was two o'clock each Sunday afternoon for $10 a month! Two o'clock on a Sunday afternoon! What seemed to be a horrible time turned out to be God's appointed time. Soon a group that averaged sixty-five the first six months began to meet and reach out to the folks in Dandora Estates.

The long-range strategy called for building a multipurpose building in each of the four estates. The cost of each building would be between $85,000 and $100,000 depending on the building standards of each estate area. A weekday ministry would be an integral part of meeting the specific needs of each community, that is, day care centers, health care, and so forth. The church would build a conventional worship center later with their own funds if they so desired. Our immediate strategy called for meeting community needs and having Bible studies during the week and worship services on Sundays in the multipurpose building.

I would like now to focus our attention on the day-to-day problems I encountered in ministering in an urban setting in Kenya. Obviously, some readers will not agree with my philosophy or my conclusions. That's OK.

1. *Land.* The cost of a half acre in 1980 was $41,000 in most areas of Nairobi. Some estate areas sold one-third-acre lots for $87,000. The thought of purchasing land to build a church was out of the question. The average Baptist church member in the city earned less than $150 per month. Alternatives had to be sought.

2. *Government lands.* Kenya would give land to religious bodies for as little as $155. The tract would be one-half acre and they would charge only surveying costs. Six Baptist churches in Nairobi were built in the decade of the sixties in this manner.

From 1978 until I left Nairobi in December 1982 the city council and the national government did not issue any land to any religious bodies because of political unrest. Land was a political football. Those of us who were trying to get land were never told this fact, but in March 1983 a member of the Nairobi Baptist Association was finally told that the only person who could give land to a religious body was the president of the country.

3. *Buildings.* Often buildings serve as prisons in which the good news is locked up, insulating it from the teeming masses who live around them. Alternate forms of buildings which provide weekday space for evangelism and discipleship should be found. This is my personal feeling, but the African culture runs almost contrary to my philosophy. In East and West Africa, the typical African desires to

worship in the conventional western-type church building. They will meet in a house or a community building for a short period but expect to move into a more conventional church within a few years. In the house churches we started in Nairobi, this was a continuous problem.

4. *House Churches.* Good leadership is very important, otherwise discouragement will result and the group will fall apart. Not everyone is comfortable in a small group because it is too intimate. Economically, it is hard to support a pastor with a cell group. We were constantly having to plan alternative programs for small children and subteens. These two groups always complicated our ministry to the adults. Eventually, we had to plan a time for various target groups. The fact that families will not stay with the house church much more than two years was borne out by other denominations who tried a similar strategy.

5. *Squatter settlements.* Urban areas of the Third World now accommodate over 800 million people and by the year 2000, they will have tripled in population. In Africa, urban areas will have increased fivefold. Between one half and two thirds of the present population of the Third World cities live in slums and squatter settlements. In Africa squatter settlements constitute 90 percent of Addis Ababa, 64 percent of Accra, and 33 percent of Nairobi.

Reaching new migrants was a low priority for the first two years of my ministry in Nairobi. Finally, a national pastor pointed out to me that they were the most responsive to the gospel. In fact they proved to be more responsive in the city than back in their village. The traditional guardians of customs and ideas do not exist in the city. People away from home are "off balance" and willing to listen to what they considered strange back home. I would certainly have spent more time with this group if I had it to do all over again.

What will it take to win a city like Nairobi to Christ? It will take committed men and women of every color confronting the urban dweller with the claims of Christ. The Holy Spirit has already prepared the hearts of millions in the urban world; they have a need and a desire in their hearts. Many are silently crying out for someone to assist them. And there are committed laypersons who are waiting for someone to guide them in planning a strategy to win their city to Christ. So as we look out over the cities, remember the words of our Lord, "Do not be afraid, . . . speak, . . . for I am with you, . . . for I have many people in this city" (Acts 18:9-10).

Bangkok

My next-door neighbor collects birds. Because he is a wealthy Chinese-Thai exporter, he can afford to buy any rare and exotic bird any ingenious hunter can trap in Thailand's jungles. He has spent no less than a million baht to fill his half-acre compound with cages of macaws, peacocks, talking mynahs, and other strange and wonderful birds feathered in brilliant blues, yellows, reds, and greens. Their hundreds of different songs, squawks, peeps, and chirps have made alarm clocks almost obsolete at our house. For the most part, he has operated on the principle of "birds of a feather flock together." The inhabitants of most cages are of a kind. Yet his largest cage, the one closest to us, is a hodgepodge of unclassified leftovers that range from peacocks to parakeets. Interestingly, the encaged bird community attracts twittering flocks of rice birds that flaunt their freedom all around the cages of their entrapped cousins.

Bangkok is a lot like the aviary next door. Most of its 5.5 million inhabitants were not brought here against their will (some were, and that's another sad story), but there are many strange and wonderful species among them and most are not free though their name is Thai. A few thousand Christians (Protestants and Catholics together number at most 45,000) are trying their wings of freedom in Christ, but most are still kept from a free decision for Christ by being encaged in preconceived ideas, family pressure, traditional religion, and secularism.

The Anatomy of Bangkok

All roads lead to Bangkok. Geographically, economically, politically, culturally—any way you can name—Bangkok is the heartbeat of Thailand. Thailand is a one-city country. Not one of Bangkok's rivals—Chiang Mai, Hat Yai, Chon Buri, Khorat—has a hundred thousand population. That would hardly register on the same scale as Bangkok's five million. Bangkok is a giant magnet attracting between thirty and forty thousand immigrants a month looking for jobs and a few square meters to scratch out a better life.

On the surface Thailand looks like a very homogeneous country. It is not as monolithic in culture as Japan. But compared with the Philippines, Indonesia, and certainly Malaysia and India, Thailand is remarkably united by the Thai language, culture, history, and world view. At the most remote primary school, Bangkok-Ayuthaya, Thai is the medium of instruction. A speaker of the official Bangkok Thai can communicate easily in any part of the country.

It is true that there are major differences in the dialects spoken by the common people of each region. Issan Thai spoken in the northeast is almost identical to the language of Laos. Northern Thai has retained some of the characteristics of the Thai spoken in Sipsong Panna in southwest China whence, according to tradition, the Thai originally came. Southern Thai is clipped, crisper, and is spoken faster than Central Thai. There are subdialects in almost every province. There are also strong regional identities and feelings, differences in folk dances and folk songs.

Yet there is a strong underlying Thai culture that pulls it all together and makes it valid to speak of a Thai way of life and a Thai world view. There is that uncanny ability of the Thai way of life to borrow freely from many sources, to absorb people of many races and backgrounds, and in it all to stamp the finished product as uniquely Thai.

It is not surprising that Bangkok has become a mosaic of all the tribes, classes, regions, and subcultures that make up Thailand. Two mainstreams have united through 200 years of history to form the base of Bangkok's population. The first, strangely enough, is the Chinese immigrant trader from the Dwatow area of southeast China already present in some strength when the first king of the Chakri dynasty founded his royal capital on the site of the trading village of Bangkok. The second stream is composed of all the Thai—nobility, soldiers, civil servants, hangers-on, servants—who gathered around the royal court.

From the intermingling of these two streams has come a fusion that is unique, as far as I can determine, in Asian history. Somehow the Thai culture has been able to absorb the Chinese into the Thai way of life until they see themselves as more Thai than Chinese. Yet in spite of their very real Thai consciousness, they have retained some characteristics that are observably Chinese. I would estimate that this new kind of Thai is the largest single segment of Bangkok's population, and it carries an influence far beyond its numbers.

The Bangkok mix includes the predominant Chinese Thai (for want of a better name), the pure Thai, and a large number of Chinese—perhaps 10 percent of the whole—who choose to maintain a distinctively Chinese way of life in certain Bangkok enclaves. Add to this mix the constant immigration of up-country people. Like birds of a feather they flock together. There is a slum that is mostly composed of taxi drivers from Ubon in the northeast. There is a housing development in which most of the upwardly mobile residents are from Chiang Mai or Chiang Rai in the north. In another area there is a *soi* (lane) where most of the residents speak Southern Thai. On a particular construction site, most of the workers may speak Khmer among themselves coming as they do from among the one million ethnic Cambodians who are citizens of northeast Thailand. My neighborhood is composed of Thai Chinese, and they stay behind their high, secure fences. Yet as we walk through the streets in the evening, the people enjoying the cool of the day along the streets invariably speak Issan. On the other hand, there are neighborhoods where people from many different areas of Thailand are thrown together, much like the birds in my neighbor's largest cage.

What does this mean for evangelizing Bangkok—"evangelism that results in churches" as Dr. Keith Parks often says?

A Strategy for Reaching Certain Groups

Baptists in Bangkok have aimed at certain distinct groups in the city, somewhat by happenstance at first and in recent years more by design. Since the first missionaries were refugees from the communist takeover in China, it was natural that their first work was started among Chinese. From those early beginnings have come three strong Chinese churches, Grace, New Hope, and Antioch. However, these churches have found that as their members became more Thai in culture and especially as the young people grew up and attended Thai-language schools (no Chinese-language schools are permitted), they have moved toward more and more use of Thai in worship services.

As we began to work with the Thai, we discovered two things: Chinese Thai were the most responsive, and young people, especially students, were the group most willing to make an open commitment to Christ.

Consequently, one group has become the dominant element in Bangkok Baptist churches. That group is the Thailand-born ethnic Chinese. Identifying themselves as Thai, they still retain a strong imprint of their Chinese heritage. They absorbed a great deal of Thai culture, but they are not nearly so bound by Thai religious and cultural tradition as pure Thai. Thai gentility has smoothed off the rough edges of the Swatow Chinese culture, but they still betray the hard Chinese drive to achieve which Thai Buddhist fatalism often stifles. They have one foot firmly in the Chinese culture and the other firmly in the Thai. Whereas Chinese churches which have clung to Chinese language and culture as the heart of their church life have not grown much, "Thai" churches which have gathered in these Thailand-born Chinese have become Bangkok's most dynamic churches.

Young people, especially students, have been another important factor in the growth of Bangkok Baptist churches. Immanuel, our oldest and largest Thai church, was started in the same rented building as the Baptist Student Center. After both church and center moved to other locations, the student center continued to lead students won to Christ into churches. More recently, New Vision Church, a vibrant, growing church formed by a nucleus out of another church, is meeting in the student center building gathering in students won there. Immanuel has opened a student hostel near a university with the hope of discipling students and starting a new church. A missionary couple assigned to on-campus evangelism at nearby Ramkhamhaeng University, Thailand's largest, have encouraged this hostel and church. Another missionary couple was preparing in late 1983 to begin on-campus evangelism at one or two more of Bangkok's seven universities.

In addition to the Chinese, Chinese Thai, and students, Baptists have tapped into other Bangkok people groups through the years.

Before 1971 most of our churches were started by renting a building, assigning a missionary family and, where available, a seminary student to work there. Almost all were begun with a program of English teaching and worship services. The successful ones were established by winning students and managing to hold on to them through the traumatic life passages of finishing school, getting a job, marriage, and starting a family. In 1971 we decided not to rent any more "chapels" even though we did not have much of a plan for beginning new work to take the place of the old pattern. We had an ideal of "house churches" and nonsubsidy from the start but no strategy for starting new churches in this manner.

The Emergence of Bangkok Urban Strategy

Between 1975 and 1979 a plan was developed by a group of Bangkok missionaries and some Thai leaders called the Bangkok Urban Strategy (BUS). It sought to bring together all the elements necessary for beginning a new church in a comprehensive, connected strategy. Some of those elements that developed were these: the use of existing churches as a base; discipling and training teams in the churches as church starting teams; aiming at target neighborhoods; surveying those neighborhoods to determine ministry needs; "climatizing" those neighborhoods through regular visits of the team to distribute tracts, correspondence courses, film evangelism, and other ways; initiating ministry groups meeting specific observed needs in the community; starting evangelistic Bible studies; conducting a ten-week discipleship "survival" course for new believers; and eventually establishing a worship group meeting weekly in a home in the neighborhood.

BUS helped us to get off dead center. Seven years after its inception in 1976 no great miracles had occurred and Thailand had still proven to be a country where church growth is painfully slow. Yet in 1983 there were 16 churches related to Southern Baptist work, more than in any other denomination. Add to that six other growing neighborhood groups and the nine Chinese churches related to American Baptist work, and Baptists have 31, almost one third, of Bangkok's 102 churches. Of course, BUS is not directly responsible for all this growth, but it helped.

Other less measurable but clearly discernible changes have come in Bangkok's spiritual atmosphere over the last seven years. Again BUS was by no means responsible for all of these, but it had some effect. There is a changed attitude: people say, "We can start new churches," and "Bangkok just does not have enough churches— only 100 for 5.5 million people." In 1982 it was estimated that nearly twenty new churches were started by mother churches, individuals with a vision, and new denominations coming in. This included what BUS was doing, of course. Another change in attitude was that one can go into Thai neighborhoods and homes and be received. Before, many church leaders had said that was a cultural "no no." BUS helped show that Thai people, on the contrary, like to welcome guests.

Over the last seven years, Baptists have come to see that we can start churches without a large outlay of money. Call them "house churches" or whatever you will, it is not beyond the faith and ability of any church to start daughter churches in a new neighborhood. The problem of providing a meeting place in the big city still exists when the group begins to grow. The time comes when space becomes a problem or when the group needs to get out from under the dominance of one family. One of the new churches, Huay Kwang, is meeting in a large apartment. Macedonia has managed to rent a storefront building with their own offerings. Canaan Church is paying back a loan to the Baptist Foundation Loan Fund which enabled them to purchase their own building for a combination meeting place and pastor's home.

A further change in the 1983 scene was intensified discipling and leadership training with the focus on leaders who were directly involved in the work. This has led to the acceptance of a "tent-making ministry" as one option for developing new work. In mid-1983 there were over 100 enrolled in all the departments of the

Baptist Seminary's new programs, many in extension centers all over Bangkok. A regular training program was in progress for neighborhood teams in the "We Care For You" organization that has grown out of BUS. The Thai version of MasterLife was introduced in 1982 and by the fall of 1983 was meeting an enthusiastic acceptance from pastors and other leaders.

Two other changes perceptible in the churches of Bangkok are clearly the gracious work of the Spirit of God in answer to prayer. During 1982 and 1983 word came from many parts of the world that Christians were burdened to pray for Thailand. During this period, an intense hunger to know the Word of God became evident among Thai Christians. Just announce an in-depth Bible study almost anywhere and you would get a roomful. Another change in the spiritual climate is a confidence that Thai people can be won; they will make decisions for Christ and they can be discipled.

This optimistic view is affirmed in the encouraging and prophetic message of Pastor Boonkrong Pitakanon. His cancer has been in remission for more than two years as thousands in Southern Baptist churches around the world and in Thailand prayed for him. In late 1983 he proclaimed more vigorously than ever: "I believe we are going to see millions of Thai people come to Christ. The day will come when there will be a church in every village, every township, every district, and every province of Thailand!" He believes Bangkok should have 1000 churches by the year 2000 and has challenged his church, Immanuel, to start one a year toward that goal.

One result of BUS has been a mixed blessing. Any change can bring negative as well as positive results. For the first time with BUS, Baptists had a group of people committed to starting new churches in Bangkok. This gave them a close comradeship in this cause. However, for some pastors and church leaders as well as for some of their fellow missionaries, the BUS closeness which sometimes appeared to be exclusiveness became a problem. Realizing this in early 1983 and not wanting a blessing to become a stumbling block, the missionaries in BUS decided to "let BUS die" as a missionary organization. The neighborhood groups and the strategy would go on. The Thai-led organization "We Care For You" would continue its work. But the form of the missionary team would die in order for its place to be taken by something broader, more inclusive, and hopefully more effective.

At this writing the question is: What will take its place? An "Evangelism Forum" of interested Bangkok Baptist missionaries has been formed. But we need to mobilize all the strength of all Christians in Bangkok: the churches, the pastors, leadership, missionary force, mission institutions. How can we strategize, plan, and work together to do the absolute maximum that Baptists and their Christian co-workers can do in Bangkok to make disciples and start churches?

Baptists have a great stake in Bangkok. For 150 of the 200 years of Bangkok's existence, some Baptist witness has been here. One third of Bangkok's Christian churches are Baptist: a solid base. Over one half of Southern Baptists' eighty missionaries in Thailand live and work here. Far over half of our institutional strength is here. Thirty-three years of experience, of which seven years have been spent experimenting with a strategy for planting churches in Bangkok, can be drawn on and used. How can we let God have full control of all he has to work with and discover his "multiple strategies" for Bangkok in the years ahead?

Singapore

Background

The seed for the development of an urban strategy in Singapore was sown in 1970 by Dr. Francis DuBose of Golden Gate Baptist Theological Seminary. In a research report entitled "An Urban Survey of Singapore," DuBose recommended that the mission employ an urban specialist to assist in developing a strategy to reach this city. The Baptist Mission (the organization of Southern Baptist missionaries serving in Singapore) responded to this recommendation on August 3, 1971 when they requested the Foreign Mission Board to appoint an urban missions specialist to Singapore. Three and a half years later, in February 1975, Ralph Neighbour arrived in Singapore as an urban strategy specialist to lay the foundation for what we now know as the BCUS, that is, the Baptist Centre for Urban

Studies. (A more appropriate title would be the Baptist Centre for Urban Evangelism.)

After considerable research and consultation, Neighbour proposed an urban strategy which the local convention accepted in June 1975. The sophisticated and complicated strategy began with the climatization of Singaporeans through a "booktree" ministry, correspondence courses, and friendship groups. The friendship groups were designed to introduce non-Christians to their Christian neighbors through popular secular minicourses. These ministries were intended to channel people into home Bible studies and house churches.

Neighbour returned to America in 1977, and from 1978 to 1980 the Baptist Mission tried to continue the program that he initiated. In 1980 several evaluations were conducted in an attempt to instill new life into the program. The most significant of these was the Cost Accounting Evaluation. This evaluation analyzed each phase of the program as to the purpose, the results, and the costs. The results showed that the institution was doing a lot of "good things" but spending a lot of money to produce few results related to the purpose of the institution. The report recommended retaining the purpose of the institution but scrapping the unproductive areas and initiating a new round of research and program development related to church planting. These recommendations were accepted by the local convention and Baptist Mission, and I was invited to come to Singapore and lead in the restructuring of the strategy.

Program Design

The first step in restructuring was to discover the obstacles to planting and sustaining new and growing churches. A banquet was held for church and convention leaders and missionaries to evaluate why the churches were not starting new work and how the Baptist Centre for Urban Studies (BCUS) could assist the churches in this process. The reasons given for the failure of the churches to start extensions were: (1) lack of vision; (2) lack of adequate leadership; (3) financial burden; (4) problems in finding locations; and (5) lack of commitment by church members. When asked what the BCUS could do to assist the churches in starting new extensions, the leaders said we should: (1) motivate the churches to start new work; (2) assist in training church leaders for this task; (3) help find locations for starting new work; and (4) produce materials needed for motivation and training.

From this information and other input the strategy began to take shape. It was clear that the primary emphases would be church planting and training, undergirded by extensive research. The methods would have to be significantly simplified, and we would have to become increasingly church centered. Whereas earlier, the churches were asked to assist the BCUS in starting extensions, we were now asking how we could assist the churches in developing their own unique strategies.

As the BCUS strategy began to emerge, we had to get ourselves organized. At this point, Management by Objectives (MBO) was implemented. Detailed goals and subgoals were established by the Evangelism Department of the Singapore Baptist Convention, the governing body of the BCUS. An MBO workshop was held to teach Baptist Centre for Urban Studies personnel how to translate institutional goals into specific job targets. With an emphasis upon spiritual gifts, the church planter and BCUS Coordinating Committee agreed upon responsibilities that the church planter would be willing to be held accountable for during the coming year. Continuity is provided for in the program as the annual goals and priorities are part of a three-year plan which is updated annually. All the goals and priorities are related to the Southern Baptist Convention's plan of "Bold Mission Thrust."

Key Principles

Any effective program has some underlying principles that are essential to its success. Three principles seem to stand out in our restructuring of the BCUS and have been instrumental in the success of our urban strategy.

Motivation. No matter how sophisticated and well designed an urban strategy, if people are not motivated to use it, then it will not produce significant results. As a starting point, we began spending significant portions of our time getting back into the churches and establishing reciprocal relationships with leaders and church members. We also refused to impose a specific strategy upon the churches. The autonomy of the local church was emphasized as well as the need for each church to establish its own unique strategy based upon its resources and character. We worked to motivate the churches to start new work and promised to assist them in developing and implementing their strategies. In order to stimulate their efforts, we offered ten different approaches to starting new work that could serve as models.

Another area of motivation involved the ownership of the BCUS. On paper, the BCUS was a convention project. Yet everyone knew that the key leaders were missionaries; over 80 percent of the funds were from the mission, and the mission retained the right to veto any decisions made by local bodies in regards to the institution. It is not surprising that Singaporeans were not willing to invest their lives in a program controlled by someone else. The reversal of the abovementioned factors has been an important element in motivation for the BCUS. The BCUS is now in the hands of Singaporeans which leads us to the second factor—nationalization.

Nationalization. One of the greatest obstacles to the success of the urban strategy was the domination of the institution by the mission. The mission wanted local involvement, leadership, and nationalization, but nothing was happening. The road to success came about through determination, hard work, prayer, and a lot of trust. When nationalization started, many nationals said, "I've heard all this before, but nothing ever happens." Many measures were incorporated to cut costs so the nationals could reasonably afford nationalization. Nationals were accepted as equals and reciprocal relationships were established. We gave authority to the appropriate local bodies and worked for credibility. In April 1982 Rev. Johnson Lim was employed as the associate director, and after a year's training he became director. Another seminary trained worker became a key staff member, and more local staff are planned. A vital part of nationalization and motivation is financial support. In 1980 13 percent of our budget was locally funded, and in 1983 54 percent of our budget was locally supported.

Teamwork. Beginning in 1981, the BCUS was managed by a coordinating committee. The BCUS director, the church planting coordinator, and the director of training formed this management team. Although the director was the leader of this team, decisions were made by consensus. Significant progress has also been made in developing teamwork among the church planters.

Another aspect of teamwork involves a reciprocal relationship between the nationals and missionaries. The basic responsibility for reaching Singapore belongs to Singaporeans. We have emphasized this. As missionaries, we are here to assist and work together with Singaporeans in reaching Singapore for Christ. Singaporeans are now leading, and missionary involvement is at the request of the institution and convention. Both parties are in the learning process and the relationship is beneficial to all.

Church Planting

The basic purpose of the Baptist Centre for Urban Studies is to assist the local churches in planting and sustaining numerous new worship units among all the peoples of Singapore with a priority on responsive areas. The scarcity of land on this small island makes the creation of new traditional churches impossible. In some ways, however, this is a blessing. We emphasize "worship units." A worship unit may be defined as the primary worship service for a specific congregation or portion of a congregation. This includes multiple language services where one church has a Mandarin/Cantonese service at 8:00 AM, an English service at 10:00 AM, another English service at 12:00 noon, and a Tagalog (Filipino) service in the afternoon. We would refer to these as four worship units. In the last few months, two of our Chinese-language churches have started new English-language services, both of which are intended to be independent churches at the appropriate time.

Worship units also include new extension churches (our number one priority) that are begun in hotels, YWCA halls, homes, or any other place they can find to meet. Another type of worship unit that holds much promise is a church satellite.

All worship units are begun in conjunction with a mother church, including pioneer work in remote parts of the island. The BCUS does not start new work on its own initiative. Just as it is part of the Christian's basic nature to reproduce other believers, it is the nature of the church to reproduce itself.

The emphases upon worship units, motivation, and so forth are all a part of our strategy. But when we talk about strategy at the BCUS, we are talking about a coordinated plan for providing an opportunity for all the peoples of Singapore to hear the gospel, respond in faith, and be discipled. The primary thrust is on the responsive segments of our society. The secondary thrust is on people and language groups that are relatively unresponsive and have limited opportunity to hear the gospel.

Our established churches are all located in a residential ring that surrounds the central business district of Singapore. The people of Singapore, however, are being relocated in an outer circle of government-housing estates called new towns. This drastic shift of people creates a "window" of responsiveness to the gospel. The first two of these large new towns are already complete. In the past two years we have begun new worship units in these new towns, yet we arrived two to four years after the new towns had been virtually completed and established. The eight remaining new towns are in varying stages of development, and each of these has been given a priority for new extension work.

This massive people movement is now in full swing and will be a significant factor regarding responsiveness to the gospel for the next ten to fifteen years. Thus, there is an urgency to proclaim the good news to these people while the "window" of responsiveness is open. There has never been and may never again be an opportunity of this magnitude for Christians in Singapore.

As part of our ongoing research, we plotted the addresses of every Baptist church member in Singapore and followed the movement trends. The churches who had members moving into each of our top priority areas for new work were identified. Then we shared with these churches the need and opportunity for starting new work in these responsive areas where they already had members to form a core group. In some cases we are able to send a missionary to assist in starting this new work, while in others we are not. Numerous approaches to providing leadership for these groups are currently being explored.

Our responsive work primarily involves English-language groups, but our strategy does not limit us to this area alone. Much of the work of the BCUS in the next few years will be in Chinese languages. There are some indications of new life in this area, and the fact that there are 600,000 people in Singapore who only speak Chinese makes it imperative that we move forward. Work among the Tamil-speaking Indians, Thais, Filipinos, Japanese, and others are also included in our present three-year plan.

As mentioned earlier, each church in Singapore is encouraged to develop its own unique strategy or approach to starting new work. As we work with these churches, we also encourage them to take into consideration our overall plan for the city. In a recent church growth conference, this plan was presented to key leaders from all our churches during a three-day conference. The attitude toward cooperation is high.

As we assist churches in developing their approach to starting new work, we present several possible models to serve as guidelines. One of our more successful models has been to train ten to fifteen people commissioned by a church to go out and begin a new extension. Queenstown Baptist Church used this approach to start the New Life extension church in 1977. Now in 1983, that same extension church is starting another extension church in our third priority area with some of the same people that began the original extension. There are many variations of this approach, all of which involve a worship service from the beginning. Last year, one such team decided not to begin with a worship service and after several weeks of difficult work determined that the worship experience is vital to reaching people. This seems to be the case in the Singapore context.

As mentioned earlier, another model involves multiple-language congregations. There are many languages and dialects in Singapore.

We have emphasized homogenous groupings, and due to the space problems these new language congregations are often begun at the same church. In the implementation of language work, assistance is needed by our churches. The design for meeting this need is to create a multilanguage, multinational institution. Our Southern Baptist missionaries work primarily in the English language, while the three-year plan envisions missionaries from other countries working with the BCUS to reach their own ethnic group in Singapore. As much as possible, these missionaries will be supported by Baptists in their own country. The Chinese-language work will be primarily led by Singaporean church planters or home missionaries.

Another form of a new worship unit is simply multiple worship services. This has been important in Singapore since space is at a premium and many of our new churches are worshiping in small areas. We have found that these small groups reach the saturation point quickly and stagnate if they don't begin a new worship service. A number of our churches now have multiple services in the same language.

Two related models are the Care Group and Home Bible Study models. The Care Group is basically a Singapore expression of the Korean home cell groups. In 1981 the BCUS sent a team to Korea to study the home cell structures. In 1982 a *Care Group Training Manual* was written to assist in the development of this concept in Singapore. Although the concept is still under development, about half of our churches are experimenting with this evangelistic approach. The Care Group provides a tremendous opportunity for the development of new extension churches. As a Care Group grows in an area beyond the general ministry of an already established church, it can be nurtured into an extension and a new church. A number of churches are interested in this model although no extensions have actually begun from this model as of this writing.

The Home Bible Study model is basically the same as the Care Group model although without the previous involvement of the Care Group. There are several Home Bible Study groups that intend to develop into extension churches; however, this traditionally effective approach has not yet proven effective in Singapore.

Another model that needs a few more years for development is the satellite concept. The First Satellite Baptist Church, of which the author is a charter member, is now beginning its third satellite. The basic idea is that a church expands through multiple worship units in different locations. This is basically a church with neither a building nor any intention of having one. Now with a Singapore pastor and five lay preachers, the future is promising for this young church.

It is virtually impossible to find a group of ten or more people from a church to start an extension in some areas of Singapore. In this case we look to pioneer work. This involves a missionary and a few dedicated workers from a church to travel to an isolated area for the difficult task of starting new work. A Southern Baptist missionary recently came to Singapore to lead out in this area.

Training

During the program development stages in 1981, the churches consistently asked for assistance in leadership training as a prerequisite for church planting. Our response to these pleas was the creation of the Baptist Training Institute (BTI). The purpose of this program is to provide basic practical training opportunities for Baptist leaders committed to church extension ministry. The BCUS's response to this need was a key step in establishing our credibility with the churches. Although this lay-training program is in its infancy stages, the future looks bright.

BTI courses are self-learning systems designed to be taught in the local church context. Although only six courses have been written and three of them are still in the first field test edition, the first year (1982) saw an enrollment of over 350. This figure was surpassed during the first half of 1983.

Specific training is also provided for church-planting teams preparing to start new extension churches. Each church receives individualized instruction since each church has its own approach.

An exciting new area of training involves a unique relationship with the Singapore branch of the Baptist Theological Seminary in Malaysia. The seminary students desiring to become pastors are assigned to the BCUS for their field work. It is hoped that an apprentice program can be developed using experienced pastors or missionaries as advisors while the students are involved in various types of extension work. Through their involvement with the BCUS, it is hoped that the unique resources of the BCUS can give them specific competencies in urban church planting and pastoring.

Conclusion

These few pages can only serve as an introduction to our urban strategy in Singapore. Although the BCUS has been uniquely designed for the Singapore context, it represents a reproducible model in many ways. The concept of an institution to assist the local churches in an overall urban strategy is certainly valid. The emphasis on research and program development is also essential for any workable urban strategy. Without proper management and teamwork, any institution will have difficulty producing significant results. Without an appreciation for the autonomy of the local church and the motivation of people, involvement will be limited. The relationship of training cannot be neglected if the initial results are to be sustained and the gains are to be conserved. If missionaries are involved, a reciprocal relationship must be established from the very beginning with the real leadership in local hands.

The Baptist Centre for Urban Studies is still an infant. Still, the results of the last few years are dramatic. In 1979-80 there were thirty worship units in Singapore. In mid-1983, there were forty-eight. Looking towards the future the Bold Mission Thrust long-range plan for Singapore envisions 400 worship units and over 40,000 (there are now less than 4,000) Baptists by the year 2000. If the flexibility and direction of the last few years continue, these goals will certainly be reached.

Note

1. *World Christian Encyclopedia*, David B. Barrett, ed. (New York: Oxford University Press, 1982, p. 434.

7

Reaching the Cities First: A Biblical Model of World Evangelization

Ervin E. Hastey

An urban imperative hangs heavy over the church. At the beginning of this century only about 13 percent of the world's population lived in cities, but now the level has increased to 41 percent and soon over half of mankind will be urban dwellers. This dramatic change must affect our mission efforts because it is now impossible to think seriously about reaching the world with the gospel of Christ without reaching the cities.

The tasks before us in the cities are staggering because they are so many. Some 240 cities have a population of one million or more, 500 have at least 500,000 persons, and an incredible 2,200 cities are over 100,000 in population. The Great Commission of the Lord Jesus Christ compels us to go into these huge cities and to plan strategies so that none are without a gospel witness.

Our reaction to the numbers, the problems, and the great need is often to cry, "Can the great urban masses be reached for Christ today? And if so, how can this be done?" In answer, Christian leaders and mission practitioners are fortunate to have a model already prepared for their task described in the Bible. The city has a most important role to play in God's dealing with persons in both the Old and New Testaments. The extension of the church of Jesus Christ as presented in the New Testament largely centers in the cities of that time. They were the centers of proclamation, witnessing, church planting, and missionary activities. Political leaders established great cities and religious leaders made them the focal point of their activities.

For many reasons the Christian emphasis on proclamation and

witnessing shifted historically from the cities to the rural areas. Even today many Christian groups have a rural mind-set and harbor fear, suspicion, and disdain for the cities. There is an urgent need for churches to recapture the vision and spirit of Christ of the important role the cities play in the redemption of the world.

The apostle Paul began his ministry at the very time great cities were being established. His three missionary journeys indicate that he spent virtually his entire ministry in the cities. He had the greatest missionary vision recorded of any follower of Jesus Christ. His objective was to reach the entire world with the gospel of Christ. His strategy centered on reaching the cities first and using them as bases for the extension of the divine message of redemption through the churches he established.

Jesus certainly had a strategy for reaching the world with his redemptive message. It was clearly set forth in very brief form in his commission to his Church in Matthew 28:16-20. His entire ministry was dedicated to the proclamation and teaching of his gospel and to the training and equipping of his disciples to reach the world. He was the perfect model of his commission.

The entire life of Jesus was related to the city. He founded the church in Jerusalem and commissioned it there for its worldwide mission. The gospel message was proclaimed through the cities and the aggressive spirit of evangelization was born there. Jesus went throughout the villages and cities in his ministry preaching, teaching, and healing (Matt. 9:35-36). Francis M. DuBose notes that Jesus was born in the city of Bethlehem, grew up in the city of Nazareth, died, and was resurrected in the city of Jerusalem. He loved the city and wept over it. The city was the context of his ministry.

DuBose also points out that Jesus commanded his disciples to tarry in the city of Jerusalem until they were endued with power from on high (Luke 24:49).[1]

After Jesus ascended into heaven, his disciples returned to the city of Jerusalem with great joy and were continually in the Temple praising God (Luke 24:52-53). They were at home in the great city of their time and carried out their mission in its context.

Christian Witness in First-Century Cities

Jerusalem

In God's wisdom and time the nations of the world were brought to Jerusalem, and the redemptive message of Christ was proclaimed to them (Acts 2:1-47). About 3000 people received him and were baptized into the church. God was preparing his messengers for a worldwide missionary enterprise when the time for their dispersion to all nations would come. The great city of Jerusalem was the proving ground and launching pad of the gospel for the world. God would use her to speed world redemption on its way. His message and messengers would flow out of her to the ends of the world. These messengers would proclaim, witness, and plant churches in all the lands of the world.

Pliny the elder called Jerusalem "the most splendid city not only of Judaea, but of the whole Levant."[2] It is also pointed out that Jerusalem was a city of schools. There were 480 synagogues and each had a school building. Instruction was free of charge. Paul was privileged to study under Gamaliel in Jerusalem.[3]

It was also the religious capital of the world, especially for the Jews. This fact brought within her walls multitudes of people every year. Gerd Wilk states, "The Feast of Passover at the time of the first full moon in spring (at our season of Easter) always brought together great masses of people. We know from a later period, in the time of the Roman emperor Nero, that 265,500 lambs were sacrificed at one such festival. This would indicate that close to three million pilgrims could have been in Jerusalem at one time."[4] Jerusalem housed God's ark and later his Temple. She was the beginning point of the Great Commission of Jesus. "But you shall receive power when the Holy Spirit has come upon you; and you shall be my witnesses both in Jerusalem and in all Judea and Samaria and to the end of the earth" (Acts 1:8).

Jesus' own earthly ministry terminated in Jerusalem. After three years of incessant trips of preaching, teaching, and healing, and after having sent out the twelve and the seventy, he came to his triumphal entry into the famed city (Matt. 21:1-11; Mark 11:1-10; Luke 19:29-

38; John 12:12-19). It had been prophesied in Zechariah 9:9 in these jubilant words, "Rejoice greatly, O daughter of Zion; shout, O daughter of Jerusalem, behold, thy King cometh unto thee: he is just, and having salvation; lowly, and riding upon an ass, and upon a colt the foal of an ass (KJV)." The Servant-King had come to begin his reign and to forewarn this great city of its sin and destruction for rejecting God's redemptive message.

During this week, he cleansed the Temple (Matt. 21:12-17), cursed the fig tree (Matt. 21:18-22); had his authority questioned (Matt. 21:23-27); spoke three parables (Matt. 21:28-32; 21:33-46; 22:1-14); severely denounced the Scribes and Pharisees (Matt. 23); left the Temple with his public ministry completed, and awaited his crucifixion which would occur three days later. His redemptive mission would culminate in Jerusalem, and the first great Christian church would be established within her limits. God was in Christ in this great city to effect his redemptive purpose in the world.

The apostle Paul serves as a perfect model for world evangelization by reaching the cities first with the gospel. He visited at least thirty cities on his missionary journeys and used a number of them as principal centers for missionary expansion. His vision of Christian world conquest had no limits. His world vision led him to make any sacrifice necessary to extend the gospel and Christ's church to the limits of his world.

The Book of Acts is indelibly marked and divided by three cities: Jerusalem, Antioch, and Rome. Jerusalem represents the first great Christian center for the expansion of the gospel. Antioch was the Gentile church center used so mightily of God to extend his kingdom on earth. Rome was the political and administrative center of the ancient world. Nero was on the royal throne; Paul arrived there in chains but declared that the gospel was not chained (2 Tim. 2:9).

The cities of Asia and Greece were large and important centers. Wolfgang E. Pax stated, "In contrast to the rural countryside of Israel, which had only small townships, here large cities dominated; by the beginning of the Christian era their number reached 330."[5] All of these cities had temples, gymnasiums, city halls, theaters, and marketplaces. They were centers of religion, commerce, culture, and politics and influenced their respective surrounding areas to a great degree.

Paul's ministry began when the Roman Empire was most powerful. Its goal was world domination. W. M. Ramsey pointed out that

> the Empire was trying to weld the separate nations into a great imperial unity, and to substitute the Roman idea of 'province' for the older idea of 'nation.' . . . Paulinistic Christianity offered itself as the power which alone could make the unity vital and effective. It was the soul which might give life to the body of the Empire, a body which the emperors were trying to galvanize into life by the religion of Roman patriotism, the worship of the Roman majesty as incarnated in the Emperors. It had now to be determined whether the Empire would accept the change of permanent vitality that was offered to it.[6]

The gospel Paul was preaching as "the power of God" was facing head-on the greatest political power of the time, and this confrontation was taking place in the prominent cities of that day. Ramsey stated "More able and prudent emperors dreaded the Pauline Church, because they recognized that ultimately it must be a foe to autocracy. The Christians were, in the last resort, the reforming party: the emperors felt that reform must affect their own power."[7]

No name in the history of the church except that of the Lord Jesus Christ is so important to the expansion of Christendom as is that of Paul the apostle. Acts 9:15 states, "But the Lord said unto him, Go thy way, for he is a chosen vessel unto me, to bear my name before the Gentiles, and kings, and the children of Israel" (KJV). Since Paul was called of God to be his messenger on a worldwide scale, it is reasonable to believe that he prepared him for the task.[8]

Tarsus

Paul was born and reared in a great city, a product of urban life. When Paul was in the Temple in Jerusalem toward the close of the seven days of purification, the Jewish leaders accosted him and accused him of defiling the Temple by bringing Greeks into it. Paul began his defense before them by saying, "I am a man which am a

Jew of Tarsus, a city in Cilicia, a citizen of no mean city" (Acts 21:39 KJV).

His birth in the Roman province of Cilicia as a free citizen made him a Roman citizen: he was "free born" (Acts 22:28). He had the rights of a citizen of Tarsus (Acts 21:39). Also he was a Hebrew, born of Jewish parents. He emphasized his Jewish origin, conversed in Greek, and stressed his Roman citizenship. He was indeed a "world" citizen.

Gerd Wilk noted that Tarsus was a metropolis of the ancient world, a seaport city, and a trade center, had a famous university, was the capital of the Roman province of Cilicia and that merchants and scholars from all the lands of the Mediterranean visited her and spent time within her confines. He also indicated that there was a sizable number of Jews who lived in Tarsus.[9] Without a doubt, the spirit and culture of this practical daily life in a self-governing free city, Tarsus, profoundly influenced Paul's life.

W. M. Ramsey aptly pointed out that

> the Tarsian state was more successful than any other of the great cities of that time in producing an amalgamated society in which the oriental and the occidental spirit in unison attained in some degree to a high plane of thought and action. In others the Greek spirit, which was always 'anti-semitic,' was too strong and too resolutely bent on attaining supremacy and crushing out all opposition. In Tarsus the Greek qualities and power were used and guided by a society which was, on the whole, more Asiatic in character. Tarsus was, through its nature and circumstances, the proper city. . . . It lay in the fact that Tarsus was the city whose institutions best and most completely united the oriental and western character.[10]

Wolfgang E. Pax stated,

> The Hellenistic City had, however, its social problems. People streamed from the countryside into the city where they felt uprooted and isolated. The large numbers of foreign workers coming from Greece to Asia Minor, Syria and Egypt, changing masters ever so often, were typical of the period. Insecurity and uncertainty were the

hallmarks of the life of the lower middle classes in the Hellenistic towns.[11]

This description has a surprisingly modern ring.

Paul, the evangelist-missionary-church planter called of God to lead out in reaching the world with the gospel, was prepared in a world-class city and carried out his ministry in similar cities. The ministries of both Jesus and Paul were inseparably linked to the cities of their day.

Antioch in Syria

Antioch in Syria was the city chosen by God to serve as the base for the extension of the gospel of Jesus Christ to the Gentile world. It was a city of 500,000 population and the third largest city of its time.[12]

Acts 11 tells us that the church was planted in Antioch by those who were scattered abroad by the persecution of Stephen. Some were from Cyprus and Cyrene, and in Antioch they preached the Lord Jesus to the Greeks as well as the Jews. A great number believed and turned to the Lord. The Jerusalem church sent Barnabas to Antioch to minister to this group. He saw the grace of God at work, exhorted them and "much people was added unto the Lord" (v. 24, KJV).

Barnabas then went to Tarsus and took Paul to Antioch where they met with the church for an entire year. The disciples were first called Christians in Antioch (Acts 11:25-26). Why did Barnabas go so quickly to Tarsus to get Paul and take him to Antioch to minister to this church?

Ernie Bradford said, "It was natural that he should think of Paul. Antioch in some ways was not so unlike Tarsus: it was a melting pot of races and creeds, with Greek the predominant language. Paul's knowledge of such peoples, his eloquence and his ability to communicate with all types made him an obvious choice."[13]

Bradford further stated, "Paul, familiar with dissolute Tarsus, was now confronted with one of the most profligate cities in the world. . . . It threatened with its luxury, languor and vice. It threatened with its extravagant oriental cults, its orgiastic mentality and its sexual license."[14]

Otto F. A. Meinardus quoted Edward Gibbons as saying that Antioch "with its fountains and groves of bay trees, its bright buildings, its crowds of licentious votaries, its statue of Apollo, where, under the climate of Syria and the wealthy patronage of Rome, all that was beautiful in nature and in art created a sanctuary for a perpetual festival of vice."[15]

In spite of all of the contrary forces in Antioch, the gospel of Jesus Christ, "the power of God" was proclaimed and took root in many hearts. The church was established, grew, and prospered. It soon manifested its worldwide missionary vision and zeal by sending Paul and Barnabas as its first missionaries. This movement is recorded beginning with Acts 13.

They were sent out as directed by the Holy Spirit and embarked on the first of three missionary journeys. Paul would touch over fifty-two cities and towns on these trips and plant the gospel and Christ's church in all of the principal cities. Antioch served as the base of Paul's missionary activities. The city of Antioch now had a church with a great missionary vision to serve as a base for world evangelization.

Athens

Although it is felt by many that Paul accomplished little in this city—some feel he failed completely in his proclamation of the gospel—it should be noted that he stood in her midst and openly declared the truths of God in Christ (Acts 17:16-34). He witnessed in the synagogue, in the marketplace, and on Mars Hill in this free city of the Roman province of Achaia. Although many dismissed him with a promise to hear him again, "Howbeit certain men clave unto him, and believed: among the which was Dionysius the Areopagite, and a woman named Damaris, and others with them" (Acts 17:34, KJV).

The *International Standard Bible Encyclopedia* states that Athens had over 250,000 population. It was the old metropolis of Attica and the capital of Greece. This was the seat of Greek art and science and was a university city of the Roman world. She had spiritual and intellectual influence on Tarsus, Antioch, and Alexandria.[16] No wonder the apostle Paul felt compelled to proclaim the living Christ here!

Corinth

Paul left Athens and went to Corinth where he remained eighteen months and wrote two epistles to the Thessalonians. Four years later he revisited Corinth traveling from Ephesus. It was during this last visit that he wrote his letter to the Romans. The church was strong and vigorous.

Halley says that Corinth had 400,000 population.[17] The *International Standard Bible Encyclopedia* states that it was the capital of Corinthia with three good harbors commanding the traffic of both the eastern and the western seas. The first ships of war were built here in 664 BC. She came to be the wealthiest and most important city in Greece. Corinth had direct communication with Ephesus. It was a city of wealth, luxury, and immorality—the city of vice par excellence in the Roman world.[18]

Paul began his ministry in this city proclaiming the Word of God in the synagogue every sabbath, directing his message specifically to the Jews and Greeks (Acts 18:4). When Silas and Timothy joined him, he declared Jesus to be the Christ to the Jews. They opposed him and blasphemed; so Paul turned to the Gentiles, preaching in the house of Justus, whose house was next to the synagogue (Acts 18:5-7). The Lord then appeared to him and said, "Be not afraid, but speak, and hold not thy peace: For I am with thee, and no man shall set on thee to hurt thee: for I have much people in this city" (Acts 18:9-10, KJV).

This church was made up primarily of non-Jews (1 Cor. 12:2) and was composed mainly of the lower classes (1 Cor. 1:26). After Paul's first visit the church had a marked growth.

Rome

Paul's third missionary journey took him to Jerusalem again where God assured him that he would go to Rome. He was sent in chains to Caesarea where he stayed for two years. He then realized his dream of preaching the gospel in Rome even though to do so required him to suffer through a shipwreck and to go as a prisoner. He was in his own rented house where he preached the gospel for two years. From Rome he wrote the Epistles to the Ephesians, Philippians, Colossians, and to Philemon.

Halley points out that at one time Rome had a population of at least 1,500,000 and recently discovered documents suggest that it may have had 4,100,000 inhabitants.[19]

Paul's determination to reach the world with the gospel included this great Roman metropolis, the capital of the world. Pax wrote,

> Why did Paul undertake it? The fact that he was a prisoner going to Rome under guard was immaterial, since had Paul been willing to compromise, he would not have had to go at all. Therefore, the ultimate reason must be seen as Paul's unshakable determination to reach the world's capital in whatever form, whether as a free man or a prisoner. He had clearly stated it as his aim in Ephesus when he was about to embark on his last journey to Jerusalem" (Acts 19:21).[20]

Guiding Principles

Out of the ministry and principles of Jesus and Paul, all those who engaged in the evangelistic and missionary extension of the early church in these cities and others not mentioned in this paper, come some guiding principles which will help us in reaching the cities of today's world for Christ. Today's cities are larger and perhaps more complex than those mentioned in the New Testament, but these principles are transferable to our modern urban centers.

Proclamation

In every city, the early disciples urgently and earnestly proclaimed Christ—his life, death, resurrection, and coming. The kerygma was central in their evangelistic methods.

Jesus instituted the church in the city of Jerusalem and commissioned her there. He commanded her members to be "my witnesses in Jerusalem, and in all Judea and Samaria to the end of the earth" (Acts 1:8).

Paul and his co-workers proclaimed the gospel of Christ as the "power of God unto salvation" in all the great urban centers of their time. They were the centers of political power and decision making, commercial centers, centers of education and communications, religious centers, and centers of vice and immorality. In all these cities where the gospel was proclaimed, by whatever methods, people responded positively to it, and lives were regenerated through the power of the kerygma.

Virgil Gerber stated, "The book of Acts gives us a picture of cyclical on-going evangelistic activity. In chapter 2, verses 40 through 47, we find that there was proclamation followed by conversion, followed by incorporation, followed by indoctrination."[21]

No modern city can be impacted for Christ without a bold and intrepid proclamation of the gospel of Christ; and, conversely, converts to Christ can be won in any modern city where the gospel is faithfully and wisely proclaimed by flaming evangels.

Church Planting

The disciples were not content with seed sowing alone but sought to plant fellowships of local congregations. These centers of fellowship, ministry, and outreach are an integral part of the New Testament method as revealed in the Acts of the Apostles.

The church was birthed in Jerusalem, the greatest urban center of her day. Paul and his colaborers planted churches in all of the major urban centers of his world. Francis M. DuBose said, "Paul's self-image was that of an apostle and minister, but the supreme direction of that apostleship and ministry was as a church planter. He was an evangelist, to be sure, but the fruit of his evangelistic ministry was churches."[22]

DuBose quoted Roland Allen as saying,

In little more than ten years Saint Paul established the church in four provinces of the Empire, Galatia, Macedonia, Achaia and Asia. Before A.D. 47 there were no churches in these provinces; in A.D. 57 Saint Paul could speak as if the work there was done, and could plan extensive tours into the far west without anxiety lest the churches which he founded perish in his absence for want of his guidance or support.[23]

The spiritual cells called churches which were established in and through the ministries of Christ, Paul, and others were found to be quite capable of reproducing themselves in the most hostile environment of the largest cities of their days. Modern cities can be turned toward Christ to the extent that his church is planted throughout them and fulfills his commission to "make disciples of all nations." What is needed in the great cities of today is an evangelism which results in churches.

Nurture

Follow-up in the churches of the first century cities played an important role. It was an immediate and intensive follow-up with the purpose of strengthening the believers and confirming the churches in their faith. They were grounded in biblical doctrine, personal witnessing, and missionary outreach.

The New Testament is replete with various methods New Testament Christians used in incorporating new believers into the body of Christ and in helping them grow in Christian discipleship and maturity.

Paul unceasingly prayed for the churches he established in the cities; he wrote them personal letters which included doctrinal and ethical teachings and exhortation to purity of life; he made personal visits to them to strengthen them, and he sent others such as Timothy and Titus to help them. He did not leave the churches alone in the cities where false doctrine and pagan beliefs were constantly attacking them.

In modern cities it has been found that a larger percentage of the new churches established grow and flourish when they are established by existing churches which will be in contact with them in meaningful, follow-up programs. New believers and new churches must be nurtured to Christian maturity if they are to reproduce themselves. Seed sowing and church planting without confirmation and follow-up stands no chance of impacting today's cities with the gospel of Christ. Strong churches grounded in biblical doctrine, energized by the Holy Spirit, and filled with evangelistic zeal are needed today in our urban centers.

The Indigenous Principle

New Testament churches were contextualized. They fit well into the nature of the culture. They took root in the local soil until the gospel lost its foreignness. The church in Antioch was different from the church in Jerusalem. Francis DuBose suggested that there are two basic models of church growth in Acts: Jerusalem and Antioch. He said,

> Jerusalem was a megachurch with at least 10,000 members very early in its life. Although it did reach out to Samaria, most of its growth was in Jerusalem. It had many home meetings, the ancient equivalent of the modern satellite. Despite its incredible growth and mammoth size, however, it could not mother the historic mission movement of the faith. The reason was it was never quite able to give itself away. The less prestigious, smaller Antioch church, on the other hand, had the power to release itself. It was therefore the chosen instrument for that far-reaching ministry. The Jerusalem church enjoyed enlargement growth; the Antioch church, multiplication growth—not for itself but for the Kingdom.[24]

Both of these models are needed in the larger cities of the twentieth century to reach their millions of inhabitants and those of surrounding areas.

In Philippi there was no Jewish synagogue due to the small number of Jewish inhabitants in the city. Paul and his company usually visited the synagogues of the cities, but here they went out to the riverside to attend a prayer service sponsored by a group of women. Paul preached and Lydia received the word of the Lord and was baptized. Lydia offered her home to Paul while he ministered in the city. Thus was another church established in another city of first rank within its own cultural context.

Taking into account that in many modern cities there are numbers

of varying cultures within the cities, it is necessary to let the churches
take on the particular culture of their community or neighborhood.

The Radiating Principle

Paul established churches in some major cities so that they could
serve as missionary extension centers to propagate the gospel and to
establish more churches. DuBose said, "In addition to the impact
upon Ephesus itself by the mass public meetings conducted by Paul,
the Ephesian church became a significant center whose influence was
felt all over Asia Minor. We do not have the specifics of the Pauline
strategy by which this was accomplished but the Book of Acts makes
it clear that 'all the residents of Asia heard the Word of the Lord,
both Jews and Greeks.' "[25] The seven churches of Revelation, then,
cluster around the radiating center of Ephesus. They became cells of
life that reached out to the surrounding areas.

This principle is especially important in countries where large
cities are scattered throughout the country, and these are surrounded by smaller cities and villages. Missionary centers need to be
established in the larger cities so these churches can reach out and
establish churches in the surrounding cities and villages. This is one
way disciples and churches can be multiplied.

The Multiform Principle

A variety of methods and means were used in the New Testament
cities to propagate the gospel and to establish churches. As Jesus
"went about all the cities and villages" (Matt. 9:35) effecting his
divine mission, he used various methods and strategies. He taught
and preached, healed and witnessed. His entire ministry was in the
context of a profound compassion for the people to whom he was
ministering. Peter healed in the context of public meetings as when
he healed the lame man at the Beautiful Gate in the Temple (Acts
3:1-10). The home was used as a center for teaching and preaching
the Word of God as well as for fellowship and evangelism.

Here are some of the methods of witnessing used in the first
century:

    1. the public proclamation of the divine message;

2. the teaching from house to house, in public places, in forums, and in synagogues;
3. the informal witnessing—the gossiping of the gospel;
4. the healing such as is found in Acts 3 that opened the door for sharing Christ;
5. the miracles performed by Jesus, Paul, Peter, and others;
6. the fellowshipping of the believers which testified to the love of God. People saw how Christians loved one another and were drawn to the fellowship.

In today's cities it is being found that a holistic approach to witnessing to their inhabitants is giving good results. Hospitals, clinics, schools, food centers, halfway houses, and goodwill centers are more and more using their ministries not only to proclaim and teach the gospel but also to establish churches. These multifaceted approaches and ministries are needed in today's urban centers to reach the lost with the gospel and to establish Christ's church.

The Geographical Principle

Ministry in Christ's name took place in a wide variety of geographic locations within the cities. Proclamation and teaching took place in the synagogues and in town halls; debates took place in town squares and in the forum of Mars Hill; sharing took place in small groups such as with Lydia and her group at the riverside.

Without a doubt, the home was the place most widely and often used by believers for their meetings. It is interesting to note that when Saul wanted to find Christians in numbers to persecute, he went to the homes rather than to the Temple or the synagogue (Acts 8:3).

The Holy Spirit worked in many homes on the Day of Pentecost, his presence "filled all the house where they were sitting" (Acts 2:2). The believers broke bread day by day "in their homes" (Acts 2:46). They taught and preached Jesus Christ "every day . . . at home" (Acts 5:42). The Holy Spirit fell on the house of Cornelius and used Peter in the proclamation of his word. Paul and Silas were brought into the home of the Philippian jailer where all of his household believed in God (Acts 16:34). Paul and Silas visited the home of Lydia and exhorted the brethren (Acts 16:40). There was a church in the house of Priscilla and Aquila (Rom. 16:3-5). There was a church in the house of Nympha (Col. 4:15). Also, there was a church in the home of Philemon (v. 12).

Francis DuBose aptly pointed out:

> It appears that the homes were the scene of church worship, fellow-ship, and some teaching and evangelism. The rented halls seemed to have been primarily for preaching and teaching the gospel. We, there-fore, observe that the early church assumed two forms in keeping with the norms of communications in the urban context: The mass type meeting for evangelistic impact and the small group meeting primari-ly in the homes for nurture and fellowship.[26]

Many churches that are growing and prospering in large modern cities are using the "church-in-the-home" concept to grow numeri-cally and to plant new congregations.

Dr. Paul Yonggi Cho, pastor of the Full Gospel Central Church of Seoul, Korea, listed the developing of the home cell among his seven "secrets" of church growth in Seoul. This great church had 320,000 members as of August 31, 1983. It is experiencing marked growth through home groups led by laypersons, both men and women. These home groups are composed of six to eight families or about twelve to sixteen people. When they grow beyond this number they are divided again and the assistant cell leader assumes the ministry and teaching of the new group.

Dr. Cho listed the following reasons why the home cells grow.

1. Because the group is small, members know each other and care.
2. Teaching is more personal.
3. Closer fellowship results.
4. Warmth and caring emanates from a home.
5. Sharing time is unhurried.
6. Today the home cells number 18,987 and are ministered to by 18,987 deacons and deaconesses throughout the city of Seoul.

An amazing factor is that many other churches in Seoul also have home cells covering the city, and all of the cells are growing and reaching their own communities for Jesus Christ. In one month as many as ten thousand to twelve thousand new members come into the church, and most of this growth takes place within the home cells.[27]

The Bethel Baptist Church in Mexico City was organized in 1963 with sixteen members consisting of six adults and ten youth. This church now has 1,542 members and has three morning worship services with three periods of Bible study. It also has a Sunday night worship celebration.

Bethel Baptist's outreach program is built around nineteen sectors. Within these sectors are 129 centers. Some are preaching centers, some are Bible study centers, and some are children's centers. Each sector has a pastor, most of whom are laypersons.

The program of this church is built around twelve ministries. The new members discover their spiritual gifts and ministries and are trained each week in the work of their respective ministries in the Church Training School.

There are many kinds of group activities which can be used both to establish congregations in cities and to enhance their growth. Each urban congregation needs to find a plan that will fit its cultural surroundings.

Leadership

The practice of Jesus and Paul was to find the leaders within the congregations established. Elders were appointed as well as deacons within the churches. Jesus, Paul, and others from the outside helped to equip these leaders, but the leaders themselves sprang out of the local congregations. This indigenous principle is very important for rapid and healthy church growth in today's urban centers.

The pastor of Bethel Baptist Church, Rev. Manuel Martinez, is a native of Mexico City. He is urban in his thinking and comportment. He is a part of the culture. He is the only pastor this church has had in its twenty-three years of existence. Those who are part and parcel of an urban culture have a definite advantage over those who are not.

The leadership of this church is found within the membership and trained in the church school in the culture of Mexico City and in the warm and aggressive evangelistic spirit of the church.

If the great urban centers of today's world are to be impacted with the gospel of Jesus Christ, it will be necessary to adhere carefully to the biblical models and to honor the principles of church planting and growth set forth in the new Testament. Today's cities are no more of a challenge to the gospel than were those early cities of New Testament times. The gospel preached today is the same "power of God unto salvation" as that which was available to Paul in the first century. If we will depend on this power and adhere to biblical principles, we can experience a new day for the gospel of Christ in today's great cities.

Notes

1. Francis M. DuBose, *How Churches Grow in an Urban World* (Nashville: Broadman Press, 1978), pp. 43-44.
2. Wolfgang E. Pax, *In the Footsteps of St. Paul* (Jerusalem, Tel-Aviv, Haifa: Steinmatzky's Agency, Nateer Publishing), p. 9.
3. Ibid., pp. 31-32.
4. Gerd Wilk, *Journeys with Jesus and Paul* (Philadelphia: Fortress Press), p. 14.
5. Pax, *In the Footsteps of St. Paul.*
6. W. M. Ramsey, *The Cities of St. Paul* (New York: George H. Doran Company), pp. 70-71.
7. Ibid., pp. 73-74.
8. Wilk, pp. 71-74.
9. Ibid., p. 74.
10. W. M. Ramsey, pp. 88-89.
11. Pax, p. 29.
12. Ibid., p. 50.
13. Ernie Bradford, *Paul the Traveller* (New York: McMillian Publishing Co., Inc., 1976), p. 103.
14. Ibid., p. 105.
15. Otto F. Meinardus, *St. Paul in Ephesus and the Cities of Galatia and Cyprus* (New Rochelle: Caratzas Brothers, Publishers, 1979), p. 2.
16. *The International Bible Standard Encyclopedia,* Vol. I, S.V. "Athens."
17. Henry H. Halley, *Halley's Bible Handbook,* 23rd ed. (Grand Rapids, Michigan: Zondervan Publishing House, 1964), p. 544.
18. *The International Bible Standard Encyclopedia,* Vol. II, S.V. "Corinth."
19. Halley, p. 534.
20. Pax, *In the Footsteps of St. Paul.*

21. Vergil Gerber, *God's Way to Keep a Church Going and Growing* (Glendale, California: G/L Publications, 1973), p. 21.
22. DuBose, p. 46.
23. Ibid.
24. Ibid., p. 154.
25. Ibid., p. 48.
26. Ibid., p. 56.
27. *Urban Mission* (Jan. 1984), pp. 4-14.

8

Planning a Holistic Strategy for Urban Witness

A. Clark Scanlon

In the pages of this book you have seen the nature of urbanization and evangelism in cities of the world. You have suffered with the slum dwellers, and you have observed bright spots of hope in illustrations documenting how urban dwellers find a new orientation in life through Christ. As a missiologist, a missionary, an evangelist, a pastor, or a concerned world Christian, you now raise your own core questions: How do I start a holistic ministry that impacts my city? What is the best way to draw a rapidly secularizing city to Christ? How would Christ have his people minister and witness in this city?

Each concerned Christian searches for an answer to urban strategy from his or her own vantage point. The missiologist looks for an urban strategy that equips Christians to meet the challenge of world evangelization. Missionaries need practical guidelines to help win the cities in their adopted land. The director of evangelism (with regional responsibilities) seeks a way to share the challenge of the cities with Christian leaders. Finally, the urban missionary or pastor looks for more effective ways to reach urban dwellers in their cities.

Missionary Donald M. Simms expressed this yearning for a personal answer to the needs of the city after he went to the top of Mexico City's Latin American Tower, looked out over the lights of his city, and felt stirrings in his heart that changed the direction of his life. In a letter home he wrote:

> That night as I stood looking out over the lights of Mexico City from some 40-odd floors up in the Latin American Tower, the number fell

off my lips so easily: 17 million live in the metropolitan area of the Federal District.

My suspicious mind said that such a figure couldn't be true. Else how could I explain my lack of concern? How can I live so comfortably in a city where there are so many lost people?

I had to discount the idea that the number is purely an illusion. Though Baptist work in Mexico City is stronger than ever before, geographic, political, religious, linguistic, and cultural barriers have sealed off major groups of people from the gospel.

But if the statistics are not an illusion, then I have to get back to myself. What allows me to repeat the number so casually?

I hide from myself the true dimensions of this city in which I live. I don't understand poverty or the reality of how many people starve every day. The physical and spiritual needs of the city depress me and make me feel guilty.

I have heard the statistics too often. After a while they become clichés, and finally I no longer hear them. And, increasingly, what I do not see tends to become unreal.

Since I came down from the tower that night, God has helped to make me a more understanding, caring, and witnessing person.

Simms's experience strikes a kindred note in the heart of many an urban missionary or pastor who, facing the overwhelming needs of the city, rejects despair and recommits a life to being Christ's person in their sector of the city.

This chapter deals with the development of a holistic ministry. By holistic, we mean quite simply *ministering to the whole person in Christ's name.* In Mark 12:30, Jesus told us we are to love God with heart, mind, soul, and strength—in short, our whole being. A holistic strategy today incorporates those same elements. It begins with a person's need for redemption, and seeks to impart the highest good by winning the person to faith in Christ. It does not stop with a spiritual witness but in compassionate caring ministers to other needs as well.

Establishing General Principles

Two truths about the nature of the church provide a background for the general principles for establishing a holistic strategy for a city.

First, the nature of the church as the body of Christ provides a unity on which principles of a strategy should be based. Second, as individuals become children of God through faith in Christ, they become members of the family of God. Local churches are expressions of that family relationship and should be viewed in this manner as a holistic strategy is constructed.

Christians have a mutual understanding because as formerly lost and alienated persons they have become part of the body of Christ and members of the family of God through faith in Christ. As the body of Christ, the family of God, and disciples of Jesus Christ, the church is to express its life in certain functions. These essential functions provide guidance for the development of specific holistic strategies.

Sharing the good news of Christ means calling persons to repent, trust Christ, and become members of his body. Acts 20:21 affirms repentance and belief as the beginning place for becoming a whole person. The regenerate become members of the body of Christ and are to work in a local church fellowship. Some of the most effective examples of urban ministry take place where the church opens itself to become a substitute for the natural family.

A modern example of the church as a family occurs in Panama City, Panama. There, Baptists from the San Blas Islands find fellow islanders in a Cuna-speaking church in the capital city where nearly a third of Panama's population live. Persons temporarily in town or living in a very different culture can find old friends or acquaintances and enjoy a few moments in their mother tongue by participation in the family nature of a church.

In a similar fashion in Paris, France, on Sunday afternoon, Chinese from restaurants, businesses, and jobs all over the metropolitan area meet for Bible study and worship in a Chinese Baptist church. Persons arriving in Mexico city find fellow believers from their hometown in one of several churches. The family nature of the church expressing itself in a holistic ministry provides a key point of entry, acceptance, and contact to a person otherwise not at home in the city.

Moving from the nature of the church as the body of Christ and the family of God, we look to four general principles that can help

in the development of an urban strategy. They involve understanding a holistic approach as an expression of God's world plan, building a strategy that reflects the nature of the gospel, knowing the city,
and understanding the meaning and power of a holistic approach.

The Holistic Approach:
An Expression of God's World Plan

No truth shines forth more clearly in the Bible than the fact that
God cares for persons as persons. When King David committed
adultery with Bathsheba, the wife of Uriah the Hittite, he treated
both Uriah and Bathsheba as expendable objects (2 Sam. 11—12).
God sent Nathan the prophet to confront David with his sin and its
consequences. God underscored the fact that persons have infinite
value and not one is expendable to be destroyed for personal gain,
even if the offender is the king of the land.

God affirmed the value of persons and his concern for them in the
Book of Amos. When the poor were exploited and oppressed, God
sent Amos onto the scene to call the nation to repent, beginning at
the king's court. Amos's blunt message declared that no amount of
legal machinations can hide injustice from God who honors persons
as having infinite value because they are created in his image.

Jesus' ministry is an example par excellence of a holistic approach.
Using the words of Isaiah, Jesus described his own life and ministry
in holistic terms (see Luke 4:16-21).

> Preach the good news to the poor.
> Proclaim freedom to the prisoners.
> Give sight to the blind.
> Proclaim freedom to the oppressed.

Jesus' ministry exemplified a holistic ministry.

> Jesus went through all the towns and villages, teaching in their syna-
> gogues, preaching the good news of the kingdom and healing every
> disease and sickness. When he saw the crowds, he had compassion on
> them, because they were harrassed and helpless, like sheep without
> a shepherd (Matt. 9:35-36, NIV).

These verses express Jesus' numerous encounters with individuals. He fed the hungry, gave sight to the blind, revealed the blind spots in the self-righteous and gave forgiveness to the repentant sinners. He met each person at the point of his or her need.

A Strategy in Agreement with the Nature of the Gospel

Many voices tell the missionary and the urban minister how they ought to act and how they must provide an authentic expression of the Christian faith. Some statements are authentic and prophetic while others are political philosophies with Christian names. Calls to wholesale class hatred and attendant violence violate the spirit of Christ. Other voices distort the gospel and seek to make Christian missions no more than an expression of humanitarianism with no call to repentance and conversion.

Kenneth Scott Latourette in his monumental work *A History of the Expansion of Christianity* repeatedly shows that the methods by which Christianity is spread affect the nature of the Christianity that results. Thus those advocating violence, teaching hatred, and employing methods that deny the love nature of the gospel do disservice to the faith. With reference to the gospel, the end does not justify the means; the end determines the means.

As Evangelicals we need to see that a holistic strategy must include evangelism *and* improving community conditions. We must begin the process by first winning persons to new life in Christ and then encouraging them to become building blocks for a better society.

Knowing the City Generally and Specifically

The best urban strategist must be both theologian and anthropologist. He must discern the ways of God, but he must know how to communicate them in terms that are understandable and relevant to the city dwellers.

Knowing the City Generally. The urban strategist today can avail himself of many fine books on the urban scene. Kirk Hadaway, research director for the Center for Urban Church Studies, recently underscored the value of research in designing an urban strategy.

He noted the failure to do research may leave us open to avoidable errors.

> I also feel that a great deal more research *must* be conducted if we ever hope to deal with some of the problems our denomination is presently facing. Misconceptions are many and entire programs may be well guided by faulty assumptions. Without good research to test our assumptions, activity proceeds without the knowledge that what we are doing works or that there might be a better way.[1]

Hadaway listed three essential things that urban research can provide for Christians developing a strategy. It can provide the *facts* on the nature of the community, the needs of the people, and the development of the city. In like manner it can provide a controlled opportunity to *test*. Often pilot projects on a small scale can test the validity of a proposal before it is attempted on a large and sometimes expensive scale. Research, Hadaway said, can also reveal some *alternative ways* of doing things.[2]

Through sound research techniques we can learn much about the general nature of the city that will enable us to construct an effective urban strategy. We need to understand the makeup of the city, the ways cities develop, the meaning of industrialization, the reason for slums, and the direction of movement to the city.

Churches that minister must deal with certain problems that are not specific to any one city but are instead more general problems faced by most urban persons. The first is *loneliness,* for in the city many are far away from family and friends and are caught up in the impersonal round of city life. A Christian manager in a large American city shared a burden with a Christian friend at a service club luncheon. The manager was devastated because a woman in his office, and under his supervision, had committed suicide. Upon inquiry, he found that the secretary who worked at the next desk did not know her very well. A few more questions told the manager the woman had no close friends in the office. As he continued his investigation, the manager finally reached a sad conclusion. In the midst of a great city, the woman had no friends at all. She had become so lonely she preferred death to life. Of the several Christians working in the office, none had sensed the depths of her loneliness.

Closely allied to loneliness is *alienation*. Persons in large agglomerations can feel alienated from society and conclude they have no part in it. At first they may enjoy anonymity, but only for a while. Hostility springing from alienation can drive them to disruptive and antisocial behavior. Smearing walls, destroying property, and mugging are but three examples of alienated persons who lash out at others. The willingness to destroy property, to deface, to commit vandalism, and to harm helpless persons all express alienation. This alienation separates one from God, from self, from other persons, from values, and from the whole fabric of society. Alienation is a graphic expression of sin. The holistic strategy for a city includes reaching out to the marginal, the rejected, the lonely, and the alienated to give them a sense of community.

In looking at the general nature of the urban scene, we also observe that the city offers anonymity. Persons in large crowds, in great agglomerations of people, seem to lose their individuality and with it a sense of responsibility. Old mores—the pressure of community standards—no longer hold them in line, and many feel free to do whatever they please. Large cities like Amsterdam, Mexico City, Tokyo, New York, or London offer their prostitution, massage parlors, and sex shops. In the city few take note of one's activities, and city dwellers may develop a concept that they live in a world where they set their own rules.

The vastness and the scurrying pace of the city contributes to *depersonalization*. The person receiving the toll at one turnpike booth may seem no more personal than the electronic receptacle at another. At a dizzying pace automatic tellers replace tellers in banks, and increasing automation means that in large cities persons can live for days without contact with other persons. For the same busy urban dweller, an elevator operator becomes no more personal than the button of an automatic elevator. The beggar on the streets of Calcutta, Bangalore, Guatemala City, or Manila may become no more personal to us than the parking meter into which we drop a few coins.

On the other hand, as we seek to understand the general nature of urban life we must not miss the *strengths* and the significance of the city. The city sets the stage for the formation of trends, influence of the media, economic and political decision making. The city offers the opportunity for varied education, for cultural development, and for personal career accomplishment. Together the challenge and the need form the nature of the city.

As we examine and begin to understand this nature, we soon become aware that cities of the world are not monolithic structures but rather patchwork quilts of ethnic, economic, and language groups. Background knowledge of the city provides a base for the development of a holistic strategy. The larger task of reaching the city must then be subdivided into ways of reaching the component parts. The question becomes, "How do we reach the Lanus community in greater Buenos Aires?" rather than "How do you reach Buenos Aires?"

Knowing the City Specifically. Knowing the city generally gives Christians the insights of sociologists or urbanologists. Such background studies can aid the Christian pastor and the missionary in developing and implementing a comprehensive, holistic urban ministry. Beyond that general knowledge of the city, a concerted strategy best grows out of a specific acquaintance with the city. Roger Greenway said it well.

> The right strategy for Mexico City, Caracas, Bogota, Sao Paulo and Buenos Aires should fit the "realities of the situation" in which millions of urbanites know little or nothing of biblical Christianity, are groping for a religious experience which is meaningful and true, and who today in the circumstances of urbanization are open to evangelism as never before.[3]

In addition to providing information concerning the general nature of the city, research can provide knowledge of a specific city that can help to determine the best holistic strategy. Hadaway related the use of the research by an association of churches in Los Angeles.

> The research that goes into the development of a data report for an association involves the collection of information from a variety of

sources. Census data is needed to give an overview of what is happening to the population in an association's territory. We look at population growth or decline in the association as a whole and also try to identify areas of the association that are growing (or declining) most rapidly. Of similar importance are race and ethnicity. We show the racial composition of the area and how it may have changed over the past decade. In doing so, we try to point out various racial and ethnic populations that may merit greater attention by the association. Additional data on age, income, housing values, marital status, mobility, and so on are discussed, in each case drawing implications for ministry and evangelism.[4]

The general principle evolves that to minister one must know the city, not only generally and theoretically, but specifically and personally. As we explore some specific steps churches can take in implementing strategy, we will look at some practical ways in which they can know their city in this way.

Discussed below are areas of knowledge that will assist us in developing a holistic urban strategy. They are in the ethnic makeup, the growth patterns, the current opportunities, the needs, a survey of how the government is meeting needs, and the potential areas and methods of ministry.

Ethnic Makeup—Implementing a holistic urban strategy will normally require a study of ethnic makeup of the city. In an unpublished study of Brussels, urban strategist-pastor Ralph Neighbour found that there is great divergence in the cities. He found enclaves of Turks, Spaniards, Germans, and North Africans living in identifiable communities. They followed their customs, lived a particular family organization, and ate their special kinds of foods. Ethnic groups formed identifiable subcultures with a varying degree of awareness and receptivity to the gospel.

Each of the different component parts of the urban agglomeration of Brussels requires a different approach. Some of those component parts are immediately open for a ministry and would show a degree of receptivity. Others are most resistant at the present time. A continuing monitoring of an urban scene will reveal change and an attendant modification in receptivity.

Growth Patterns—Insights into the best approach to the city can come from examining demographics. The various communities clustering around the central urban core grow at different rates. Some localities represent the place where newcomers arrive almost daily. Both political and economic refugees may affect the growth of sectors in some cities. The refugees going into Macao, Miami, Pakistan, and Ghana produce massive changes in cities where they go. Other communities remain more stable. Still other communities are aging, declining, or transitional. Such firsthand knowledge of the city aids in applying the right strategy to the community.

Current Opportunities—Meaningful research can uncover current opportunities for witness and ministry. Practical experience has taught urban pastors and missionaries that newcomers to the city are often more responsive to the gospel than they were back in their home community or will be when settled in the city. David B. Barrett, with long years of experience with the Church Missionary Society in Kenya, has found that one of the great challenges of the African churches is to hold Christians won in the villages as they move into the city. They can provide a bridge to reaching others who are often lost to churches as they move to the city.

Pentecostals in Latin America have had notable success in providing new roots, a sense of community, and an accepting family to those who are rootless, marginated, and bewildered in the complexity of megapolis.

Needs—Research, both general and community oriented, can provide a good base for strategy by discovering needs of persons in a community. John Cheyne, the senior human needs consultant for the Southern Baptist Foreign Mission Board, said that Jesus' contact point with a person in the Gospels was the person's need. Jesus began with their perceived need for water—for healing, for sight, for bread—but he moved on to their deepest need: salvation, reconciliation with God, and the abundant life in Christ.

Where and How the Government Is Working—Careful research should take into account government programs. A church can avoid duplication of services provided by the government. It can also look for ways in which these services offer opportunity for new service.

When a new government housing area is developed, there may be plots assigned for community centers or churches.

David B. Barrett pointed out that in a number of the Western countries many of the social needs of citizens are cared for by the state. He said:

> In the Scandanavian countries, in West Germany, in France, in Britain and in the other countries there, the state provides all secular ministries for its citizens from the cradle to the grave. Free schooling, free hospitals, massive unemployment benefits and the like, all militate against initiatives in these areas on the part of the Christian churches.

While true with regard to institutional services, the need for personal ministry to the whole person in counseling, caring, personal support, and orientation will always exist for the church alert to personal needs.

Potential Areas and Methods of Ministry—With research in hand, a church or an agency can sort it out and seek guidance for direction. The Holy Spirit will guide the seeking church into areas of ministry. A survey of the community may reveal the need for literacy classes, a medical clinic, or family counseling. The servant actions of the church will also lead to witnessing activities. Neighbors who were helped by Christian friends during the 1976 earthquake in Guatemala, Hurricane Fifi in San Pedro Sula, Honduras, and the food shortage in Warsaw, Poland, are more prone to listen with attention to the Christian's witness.

Understanding the Meaning and Power of the Holistic Approach

Our nature as human beings makes a holistic approach effective. Men and women are created as whole persons. We have bodies, emotions, wills, intellects, and spiritual natures that reflect the nature of God. In sin, humankind became separated from God. That separation brought alienation from God, from ourselves, from others, and from our environment. A holistic approach is God's way of making things right again.

God's world plan is one of reconciliation. The beginning point for reconciliation is laying down arms of rebellion to be reconciled to God in Jesus Christ. That beginning point gives us the ability to accept ourselves as children of God, our world as his creation, and our fellow beings as persons to whom we can be reconciled. Reconciliation to God, to our own best selves, and to others are parts of a holistic purpose.

In carrying out a holistic ministry, the church must perform certain functions that are essential to its nature. The first is simply that of *being.* Paul speaks volumes when he challenges the Ephesians "to live a life worthy of the calling you have received" (Eph. 4:1, NIV). Some remarkable energies have been released in urban churches that come to realize they are an entire body of ministers with gifts for ministry.

The second basic function is worshiping. Christians receive the challenge to "Speak to one another with psalms, hymns and spiritual songs. Sing and make music in your heart to the Lord" (Eph. 5:19, NIV). A holistic strategy will tap the power of celebration and the joy of united expressive worship. Large churches in Korea, Chile, and Brazil combine the intimacy of house churches with periodic massive joyous celebration in large evangelistic centers.

A holistic ministry includes *proclamation.* Paul saw proclamation of the good news as the central priority of his life. "For Christ did not send me to baptize but to preach the gospel" (1 Cor. 1:17). A holistic strategy in the city will include the announcement of the good news with its message of hope, forgiveness, the cross, the resurrection, and meaning for life.

In the giant Jotabeche Pentecostal Methodist Church in Santiago, Chile, hundreds of lay preachers move quickly after the morning preaching service to the bicycle racks in one wing of the church. From the central location they go all over the city of Santiago for street preaching. During the afternoon they win some to Christ. In the early evening, often to the accompaniment of a bass drum, they enter the large structure for the evening celebration with those they have won marching in beside them. Proclamation has become the responsibility of a large segment of the congregation, and the results of the proclamation are most impressive.

A holistic strategy will not only engage in an evangelism that wins people to Christ but in a form that draws them together in New Testament fellowships. The Lausanne Committee for World Evangelism stated the goal of evangelization as "men and women who accept Jesus Christ as Lord and Savior, and serve him in the fellowship of his church." A holistic approach will include the *koinonia* or fellowship aspect of the church's life. Indeed, a part of the evangelistic success of Pentecostals has been their provision of a family for the masses, the rootless, and the new urban dwellers. Surveys of Sunday School classes reveal that most come to church to be with friends and as a desire for fellowship.

A holistic approach includes teaching. Jesus engaged in teaching (Matt. 9:35); he also made teaching a part of the mandate of the church (Matt. 28:20). The happiest Christians are growing Christians. A holistic strategy will need to provide for training and growth of teachers.

Another phase of a church's holistic ministry is *service* or *ministry*. The church follows both the example and the teaching of Christ as it ministers. In very innovative ways, churches in the Third World have ministered by buying coffins for deceased, rehabilitating drunks, seeking release of prisoners, and aiding victims of violence. There also will be occasions in which the church enters into social action. While most often social action will come about by the involvement of individual members, there will also be occasions in which the church speaks as a body.

When Jesus described his ministry to those gathered in the synagogue in Nazareth (Luke 4:14-21), he included goals like freedom for prisoners, sight for the blind, and release for the oppressed. Although governmental restrictions or the limitation of resources may exclude some types of ministry, the church is closest to the spirit of her Lord when she witnesses by both word and deed.

The power of the holistic approach appears in the fact that God through his church is reaching to the whole person with his or her needs. The church has the opportunity to demonstrate the family traits of God's family mentioned in Matthew 5 and 25:34-40. The key concept in the Matthew 25 passage is not that the righteous were saved by their good works but that the ministries so reflected their new nature that they were not even conscious of having performed them!

Taking Specific Steps

Having looked at four guiding principles, we move to these specific steps to be taken in developing a holistic strategy.

Understanding Levels of Involvement

The broadest level of involvement is that of developing a *world strategy* of witness and ministry. In recent months Christians in all quarters of the globe have expressed a marked interest in world evangelization. The feeling that its hour has come has been voiced from the United States, Brazil, Korea, Nigeria, Kenya, and other parts of the world as well.

In July 1983 Baptists of Brazil convened a World Congress of Urban Evangelism. The congress included testimonies of effective strategies, workshops, laboratory experiences, models, and case studies from various parts of the world. The international interchange gave input for concern for urban evangelization on a world basis. Some of the insights shared included the following.

- House churches meeting in homes is one of the principal ways new churches are coming into being in Third World countries today.
- The assumption that every church must have the traditional building tends to limit growth.
- Most new congregations depend on lay leadership.
- New arrivals in cities from the rural regions are responsive. The people must be reached when they have need, when they need a substitute family. Finding a family, fellowship, and a place of acceptance and celebration, they will be stalwart church members of churches tomorrow.
- The training of leaders for home study groups may be a very effective investment of time.
- A few Christian centers or large churches with buildings can

provide a resource and a celebration center for multiple small house churches.

Such insights gained in the rough and tumble of experience provide great help to those designing their own urban strategy.

A second level of strategy development in urban holistic ministry is a plan to reach a *particular city*. A strategy may be developed by a single denomination or by several denominations working together. Strategy development involves studying the city—its potential, its need—and then taking steps to reach it for Christ. Churches can provide only limited resources, but these resources added to what the local, state, and national governments do can improve the quality of life of the city as well as give a faithful witness for Christ.

Planning to reach a whole city produces many positive results. Many current examples reinforce the value of designing and implementing a holistic urban strategy. In 1955, only three Baptist churches were related to the Guatemala Baptist Convention of churches in Guatemala City. But the pastors captured a vision. Gathered together with the encouragement of a missionary, they studied their city in detail. Pastors and laypersons studied maps provided by a young architect and made a detailed drawing of areas where they wanted to start churches.

In those areas they located Baptist churches and those of other denominations on the map. Next they placed symbols on the map to indicate members of their churches. In some neighborhoods the pastors and laypersons observed a sparse distribution of their members. They found other neighborhoods in which members of several churches were holding mission services within a few blocks of each other. Pastors put the mission groups in contact with each other and targeted unchurched areas for witness. The study gave a vision, the vision resulted in planning, and the planning and work produced new churches. Today there are fourteen Baptist churches in Guatemala City.

Illustrating how a denomination can work together in urban strategy, Baptists of the state of Sao Paulo have worked together for advance. In the last four years they have organized 110 new churches, fifty-one in 1982 alone![5] The Sao Paulo Convention has a goal and a well-designed strategy to organize 1,000 new churches in urban centers of the state between 1983 and 1992. These churches will emphasize evangelism and church development, but they will also perform multiple social ministries.

The third level for designing and implementing a holistic strategy is at the *local church* level. Ervin Hastey, the senior consultant for Evangelism and Church Growth for the Southern Baptist Foreign Mission Board, said, "When people talk about social ministries in a city, they often think in institutional terms, and do not take into account the countless acts of ministry performed by local churches." The unheralded acts include helping the sick, aiding in employment, assisting one another in time of grief, teaching people to read and write. Such churches are carrying out a holistic ministry.

Designing a Strategy

According to the level at which you are working (world, national, city, or church), your responsibility includes design of a strategy to reach and win the city for Christ. Several steps will move you toward developing a practical and working strategy.

Sharing a vision. Sharing the vision is the beginning. With the conviction that God loves the city and cares about it, leaders can stimulate fellow Christians to ministry there. Jesus had a vision of the city of Jerusalem and he communicated that vision to his disciples.

If a pastor or leader can help Christians to see the challenge of the cities of their region or their own city in particular, they will engage in ministry. But "Where there is no vision, the people perish" (Prov. 29:18, KJV). The pastor or missionary will share an overview of needs, opportunities, and of Christ's mandate. In a prayer meeting one minister developed a questionnaire for his members about their community. He used both their knowledge and their admitted lack of it to challenge them to reach their neighbors.

Informing the church. To share a vision a pastor may choose to present data graphically. A church often responds positively to maps that show the neighborhood, a nearby community, and the need for a new church. If members see graphs of demographic growth, plans for new housing developments, and hear statistics about need, they have information which can stimulate them to enter a holistic ministry.

Training the people. Once people have a vision of need and of their task, they merit training to do the job. This training should not be limited to formal Bible institute or seminary training. Workshops and short training sessions for laypersons in the cities do a great deal to foster their involvement in extending work and ministry into other parts of their city. Pastors should teach their people how to conduct a Bible study and how to administer a survey. Pastors often find if they will accompany their people and model for them what they are teaching, church members will learn more readily.

The Assemblies of God Bible Institute in San Salvador has shown how students can participate in the expansion of a work when they are both trained and involved. Several hundred Assembly of God Churches today in the capital city region bear witness to the fact that training can enhance expansion.

Similarly, members of the Jotabeche church in Santiago, Chile, train by participation and apprenticeship. With increasing levels of responsibility they participate in street services, teach Sunday School classes, and finally have their own congregations that relate to the mother church. The principle of training by association is one Jesus practiced in the training of the twelve.

Implementing the Strategy

When a neighborhood has been surveyed, people stimulated and informed, and basic training given, Christians must move on to implement the strategy for a holistic ministry. The Holy Spirit must move Christians and empower them if results are lasting. Following the principles set forth, they can take concrete steps to make a holistic strategy a reality.

Taking steps to know the city. The first way to know the city is to see it as God does. Ask him to show what he wants done in it. He has a will and a purpose for the city and will reveal that plan to his children who seek his will. Conferring with those who know the city well, either as a whole or only their own neighborhood, can reveal a wealth of information.

Farrell Runyan, the Southern Baptist Evangelism and Church Growth consultant for Africa, utilized a questionnaire (developed by missionary Jimmy Maroney, then serving in Nairobi, Kenya) with those attending a workshop in several West African countries in order to get a picture of the makeup and nature of various West African cities. The questionnaire revealed the makeup of the neighborhood, the work, the churches, the level of knowledge of the gospel, and the ethnic or linguistic makeup of the city. A Liberian pastor who participated in the workshop got a new insight into his own city of Monrovia. "I have walked through my city many times to buy in the market or to go from one place to another, but I have never really seen it. I am seeing it now through new eyes." All of a sudden, the pastor really saw his city.

One help in knowing a city is to *study maps.* One type should be large in order to locate churches, plot areas of growth or ethnic concentration, and to see areas of need. If additional detail is needed on local neighborhoods, a second series of maps should be used that are detailed enough to show individual blocks or even individual houses. One young pastor in Central America placed a symbol on a very detailed map to indicate where his church members lived on various blocks. Later he assigned these members the responsibility of contacting neighbors on their block and of organizing Bible studies in their homes.

Missionary Pat H. Carter led his seminary students in Lomas Verde area of Mexico City to *survey the neighborhood* around the seminary. The survey collected information on ways in which the church and the seminary community could be of service to them. Not only has a strong church resulted that meets in the seminary chapel, but other ministries have also opened up to the church members.

Edward R. Dayton provided some wise advice: "But regardless of the particular people God has called you to evangelize, it is important to understand them as they are, as they live in the context of their needs."[6] Again Dayton reinforces the idea that understanding the people will help in the choice of the particular methodology. "The place to begin is not with the method of evangelization, but rather with an understanding of the people, whom God loves and for whom Christ died."[7]

Moving into action. There may be failures and false starts in implementing an urban strategy, but the only sin consists of not beginning. "To him that knoweth to do good, and doeth it not, to him it is sin" (Jas. 4:17, KJV). Action will involve developing a general plan. The plan should answer questions like these: How will needs be met? Who will meet them? Who has spiritual gifts and training to meet a particular kind of need? Ralph Neighbour described this action as "finding the hole in their heart and filling it." Knowing a need and praying about it will often result in a method to do something about it.

Since most of the illustrative material in this chapter came from the Western world where a wide variety of institutionalized ministries are options, missionary scholar David B. Barrett was asked to describe some of the limitations of institutionalized ministries both in some Marxist countries and in some welfare states where many traditional Christian ministries are carried on by the state and where little social action is permitted or is prohibited by law. Barrett, research officer for the Anglican community, pointed out that in many of these countries a vastly different approach must be taken.

> Enormous diversities exist in the cities of the world. It is usually taken for granted that the strategist and his colleagues have freedom to examine the ground, freedom to investigate and consult, freedom to plan, and freedom to implement the strategy with concrete programs and plans. No such freedom for Christian strategists exists in Iran's 22 cities of over 100,000 population, or in the Soviet Union's 261, or in the People's Republic of China's 117, or in other countries hostile to Christianity.

He shared the example of Novosibirsk, a great Soviet academic and scientific city in Siberia. A rapidly growing city, Novosibirsk has grown from 645,000 in 1950 to 1,470,000 today.

This city, of course, can have no foreign mission effort and is limited to one large Orthodox cathedral established in 1948. But this one church according to Barrett's study "pulsates with life and spiritual zeal." Barrett related that on Easter Sunday, the resurrection of Jesus Christ "was celebrated in this cathedral by a packed congregation of 8,000 believers." Although prohibited by law from many social ministries and from traditional evangelization activities, the cathedral in Novosibirsk stands as testimony to the power of the gospel of Christ in the city. Travelers to the Soviet Union often testify to the warm embrace and two-cheek kiss in the Christian churches. While the collecting of money for ministry is prohibited by law, Christians in the Soviet Union and in house churches in the People's Republic of China find ways to strengthen one another and to minister in ways that cannot be stamped out by legal limitations.

In closed societies and in welfare societies, Barrett believes churches "ought, instead to concentrate their efforts on ministries that the state can never supply—teaching the Christian faith, preaching the gospel, meeting for public worship, and, of course, evangelism." He concludes with sage advice, "The strategist must be prepared to show flexibility, realism and imagination as he considers such an environment."

When background studies are completed, prayer then becomes specific for direction, for opportunity, for wisdom, for the right place, and time in which to begin. After prayer comes the initiation of specific ministries. The ministries will be shaped by the nature of the gospel, the needs of the community, and the gifts of the church. They may take the form of crisis ministries, literacy classes, job training, small-group Bible studies, street preaching, tent campaigns, radio and television ministry, or a host of other activities.

Good strategies will involve many programs of ministry and outreach, and all should be evaluated by their emphasis on a common goal. According to the Southern Baptist Evangelism and Church Growth consultant in Europe and the Middle East, "We must evangelize in such a way that churches come into being and grow." Those churches become new cells of life for testimony and service that continue to go forward until the return of the Lord Jesus Christ.

Francis M. DuBose, professor of missions at Golden Gate Baptist Theological Seminary, points to two key models of growth in the Book of Acts. Jerusalem, he said, with the presence of the apostles and the early impact of the life and resurrection of Jesus became a megachurch with probably in excess of 10,000 members. Antioch, built on this base and began to reach out and to multiply. It became the pattern for churches like Ephesus. DuBose described this pattern.

> Both traditions are a part of our tradition, and we need both today. Indeed Antioch built upon Jerusalem. But Jerusalem alone is not adequate. It is the Antiochian tradition which provides us with the ultimate model of church growth. Jerusalem kept the faith—Antioch passed it on.[8]

Whatever other method is employed, we must keep this goal in mind. New Testament churches, when established, become the roots of Christianity that can produce trees and fruit. Greenway said, "Tomorrow's man [or woman] is an urban man." To reach the world for Christ, we must reach the cities.

Notes

1. C. Kirk Hadaway, "Learning from Urban Church Research," *Review and Expositor* (Fall 1983), p. 543.
2. Ibid., pp. 543-544.
3. Roger S. Greenway, *An Urban Strategy for Latin America* (Grand Rapids: Baker Book House, 1973), p. 163.
4. Hadaway, p. 547
5. Salovi Bernardo, General Secretary and Treasurer of the Coordinating Board of the Sao Paulo Convention, Oct. 27, 1982.
6. Edward R. Dayton, *That Everyone May Hear,* 3rd ed. (Monrovia, CA: Missions Advanced Research and Communications Center, 1983), p. 43.
7. Ibid.
8. Francis M. DuBose, *How Churches Grow in an Urban World* (Nashville: Broadman Press, 1978), p. 154.
Material in this chapter from David B. Barrett was sent to A. Clark Scanlon in manuscript form and has not been published.

9

Training for Urban Evangelization

Samuel M. James

The objective of leading persons in the great urban centers of the world to a saving knowledge of Jesus Christ will involve a wide variety of strategies, techniques, and methodologies. In fact, the approaches to urban evangelization are as varied as the persons who seek this goal. Effective methods are constantly being created by missionaries on the field as they adjust to a new culture and the pressures of a large city. Others need to know these methods and be trained in these techniques—to learn how to understand a culture to the point that they can create unique approaches of their own.

Much of our training deals with teaching methodology. We produce literature, audiovisuals, and technical support equipment with the presupposition that if men and women learn how to use them correctly, evangelism will occur and people will be saved. We are also inclined to place high priority on sporadic evangelistic events and campaigns which, if carried out properly, will result in great numbers coming to Christ. With this in mind, training programs gear themselves to teach the proper use of literature, how to employ technical expertise, and how to skillfully schedule events. All of this is good, necessary, and no doubt helpful. However, the single most crucial element in successful urban evangelism has to be the *spiritual* development of that human instrument which God has always used to incarnate himself in the midst of people. This ought to be true of any evangelism training, but it is most urgently true of urban evangelism.

Urban evangelism demands that all of the technical progress in communications be brought to bear if any significant impact is to be made on the huge urban centers. It requires the most skilled application of demographic and sociological studies. Goals, objectives, and long-range planning are a must. Exorbitant costs require careful budgeting and accounting procedures. The shortage of trained personnel demands well-planned and strategic placement of individuals for maximum effectiveness. All of these are the *content of training for urban evangelization.* However, unless those human instruments of the gospel are clear in their own personal identity, emotionally healthy, and spiritually committed, all of the technology and academic exercises will be just that—exercises.

We look next at some of the broad needs which are more or less unique to the urban situation. Following this section, attention will be given to several training objectives which grow out of these needs. Then it will be necessary to review some philosophical presuppositions which should control educational methodology so it will significantly impact the trainee as a person and as a professional.

Broad Areas of Need in the Urban Setting

It is necessary to define several broad areas of need in the urban environment which a training program for urban missionaries ought to address. Needs may vary from city to city. Some large cities in the world continue to have a rural character. Others have a purely modern urban character, and these differences affect the type of training the urban missionary should receive. There are, however, some common concerns which seem to be present in any urban situation.

Dealing with the *lack of adequate funds* may be one of the great unsolved problems related to evangelism in the urban setting. The problem is multifaceted. The acquisition of facilities in which to begin a program of evangelism is one of the first problems the urban evangelist has to face. Home Bible study has been taught as an innovative answer to the problem, but ultimately larger and more convenient facilities must be provided. Often the meager resources of the new group cannot begin to meet the need. Subsidy must come from some source but usually creates as many problems as it may solve for the indigenous group.

Various media efforts are another approach that missionaries learn about and may have used as pastors or evangelists in the United States. However, in Third World cities they often require huge financial reserves not available to most urban evangelists.

Living conditions of evangelists and their families can present formidable financial stress. Many missionaries in the urban setting are not native city dwellers. They have moved into the city with the purpose of evangelism. For the urban evangelist not accustomed to the city, the lack of space for the family both inside and outside the home can take its toll on the nurturing family environment. Urban evangelists and their families should come to understand city life *before* they are thrust into an environment which may combine a new language, a new culture, and an unfamiliar urban life-style.

The *multicultural character of the cities* presents a formidable challenge to the evangelist. Whether the urban area is in North America or anywhere else in the world, the fact that it has numerous and varied cultures cannot be denied. Members of one culture are often blind to another and the urban evangelist must learn how to identify cultural boundaries and how to use them to reach people for Christ. Evangelism has to be directed appropriately to the unique qualities of various cultural and language groups. Cultural considerations also impinge upon the choice of location of a church or chapel. They often affect the choice of leadership to assist in the starting of a work. The complexity presented by the many distinct cultures of any urban population cannot be emphasized enough.

Understanding and *dealing with human need* is crucial and critical in all urban areas. On the one hand, this need is expressed in unemployment, labor strife, functional illiteracy, unsanitary living conditions, crime, drugs, and a myriad of other poverty-related problems. On the other hand, problems associated with affluence, overcommitment, secular values, loneliness, depersonalization, marital and family stress can run rampant through middle- and upper-class urban society. The deterioration of the family as a unit among all classes is distressing indeed. These problems have an acute nature in the great urban centers of the world, and the missionary must learn how to deal with them in a meaningful way.

A final broad area of concern to the missionary is the *religious nature of a city.* Spiritual awareness and need are varied and often confused in the urban setting. The need for a sense of meaning and belonging in a depersonalized society makes the urban dweller vulnerable to a host of non-Christian religions, sects, cults, and other groups which address themselves to the need to feel wanted, needed, and cared for. Others, however, react against these various expressions of so-called "religion" and embrace a secular life-style.

These are just four broad needs which evangelists must face as they approach work in the urban environment. Training or preparation of the urban evangelist ought to address itself in varying degrees to these four basic problems. Taking these issues as a basis, a number of training objectives can be stated. This is not meant to be a detailed analysis but a beginning point from which a more detailed training plan can be developed.

Training Objectives for the Urban Evangelist

Strategy Planning

The challenge of working in the midst of masses of people with every kind of human need is staggering. There can be a myriad of opportunities, distractions, influences, and temptations which surround urban evangelists every day that they move on the streets of the city. Unless they undertake their task with a clear and definite understanding of what their ministry is and a strong commitment to it, they are soon caught up in a busy life without direction.

When the goals and objective of ministry are defined, then appropriate methodologies and plans of action can be tested and tried. One of the most discouraging and defeating aspects of work in urban areas is to be unable to define and affirm definite accomplishments. It is deadening to be unsure of how effective one is. When objectives are clear and methodologies are appropriate, only then can evaluation occur, revisions be made, and effectiveness be assessed.

The very nature and character of one who undertakes the life of a servant of God lends itself to a desire to minister to everyone in need wherever and whatever the need is and whenever it occurs.

This spirit and attitude are admirable. However, unless controlled in some way, the result is fatigue and early burnout. At some point one who wants to be effective over the long course of ministry has to stop and ask, "What is it exactly that I am trying to do with the life of ministry which God has given me?" This is especially crucial in the large urban setting.

The urban evangelists must know how to to work with fellow missionaries, pastors, and laypersons in planning a strategy by clearly stating their purpose and by developing broad objectives, specific goals, and relevant action plans. Skills are also needed to evaluate progress towards these goals. Management by objectives has become a proven scientific tool for effective work in most fields of endeavor. The multi-faceted life of the minister needs desperately to use this valid tool to bring order and discipline to a life of ministry. This is especially true in the urban setting where every day one is faced with monumental choices of ministry to human need. A training program for urban evangelists must equip the evangelist with the ability to manage ministry by clear and definite objectives and goals.

Personal Development

Self-Understanding. Before missionaries can begin to witness effectively to others in the urban environment, or anywhere else for that matter, they must come to a clear understanding of who they are. Any training program should provide an arena in which individuals can clarify their identities, their sense of worth as persons, and uncover and enhance the unique gifts which they bring to tasks at hand. When persons are aware of weaknesses, they can compensate for them. When persons are aware of strengths, they can develop them. With a move into a new environment often filled with currents and crosscurrents of human involvment such as urban living provides, it is necessary to have a solid self-concept which can take risks in new relationships and which can absorb defeats, rejections, and uncertainties.

Such a training program could provide opportunities to develop group creativity and interpersonal skills. It would seem that a primary prerequisite for effective evangelism in an urban setting is to be able to meet strangers and to develop meaningful relationships with them. The missionary needs to become known as a real, genuine person through whom Christ is manifested. It may be that the foremost challenge of the evangelist is the ability to utilize good interpersonal skills both in the Christian community and in the host community.

As a healthy self-concept is developed, the missionary-evangelist can allow himself to become involved in the life of a secular community where life is lived, where hurt is felt, where joy is expressed, where play is enjoyed, and where work is done. A healthy self-concept allows the urban worker to live in the midst of conflicting moral and ethical value systems without becoming unwelcome and cutoff because of judgmental attitudes. Instead of being alienated he or she is able to stand firmly, yet lovingly, in a Christian value system and thus effect change rather than being changed by the environment.

It is sad when persons are so eager for acceptance by others they allow erosion of their own values and begin to take on the characteristics of the people about them. They may find themselves more or less accepted but probably not respected. The more the urban missionary understands himself or herself as a person, the better he or she is able to remain firmly committed yet respected and loved.

Spiritual growth. Training for urban evangelism must include the development of a vital and growing relationship to Jesus Christ and the development of resources for spiritual and emotional growth.

Life in the anonymity of a large urban setting surrounded by crass secularism, permeated by nonreligious values, and constantly depersonalized makes the maintenance of a solid Christian faith difficult. Life in the urban setting can become so busy that every hour of the day is challenged with the magnitude of the task at hand. Unless there is a firm commitment to developing a deep spiritual life of personal involvement with Jesus Christ, there will be a rapid weakening and loss of spiritual resolve. Without this firm commitment it is possible to drift away from one's original purpose.

Time must be set aside for solitude, meditation, prayer, study of God's Word, and the other spiritual disciplines. The inward life affects the outward life. Busy Christians are much more likely to cut back on developing themselves spiritually than they are to cut back on the tasks they are called to perform.

Included in training must be some assistance in the establishing of a nurturing home. With the busy urban life claiming energy and time on a continuing basis, the urban evangelist needs one good place where he can step back, take a breath, and release emotions and energy. He needs a place where he can find comfort and rest for a weary soul. The home ought to provide that as a very minimum. Working on a marriage relationship and a relationship with children ought to be a cardinal part of any missionary training program.

Motivation. Training for evangelism must result in greater motivation for service. It is one thing to present the overwhelming challenge of ministry in a great urban setting in such a way that one is inspired by the reality and eager to begin. It is another thing to present the challenge in such a way that the task is seen as too staggering. Despair, distress, and frustration then set in. When the training of urban evangelists is able to present clear alternatives, valid methodologies, and a deep sense of divine commitment, then motivation is strengthened. Such training should result in enthusiasm.

Training should always incorporate elements of theory and practical application. When education is purely cognitive, then knowledge tends to become the primary goal. When education is also concerned with the application of theory, then a proper balance is achieved. It is out of this blend of cognitive and practical education that motivation for service finds its enthusiastic expression.

Personal Evangelism

Practical experience. The urban evangelist needs practical experience in witnessing and discipling under good supervision. This sounds trite and rather unnecessary to state as a training objective. However, experience confirms that academic training in the classroom may provide a vast supply of cognitive information but may do little to determine how that information is applied. The urgent need in training for ministry today is to achieve a healthy balance between cognitive education and experiential training.

To be suddenly placed in the midst of thousands of people with the objective of leading them to an experience with Jesus Christ without some kind of support and sounding board by others who have faced the same challenge is to be sentenced to a long period of trial and error. It most often results in deep anguish, disappointment, and frustration. One of the common complaints this author has heard through the years in urban settings is, "I just can't seem to get a handle on my work." Translated, that simply means that one cannot seem to arrive at good clear methodologies that work effectively. This may be because urban evangelists are too often set down in the midst of a formidable challenge with little practical supervision by those who have walked that way before.

Practical training should involve both witnessing and discipleship. One of the mistakes so often made is the separation of these concepts. It is true that they are two separate disciplines, but one is not complete without the other. Some groups have great emphasis on witnessing. They have developed good, unique methods of witnessing. But so much emphasis is placed on witnessing by a particular methodology that evangelists feel that when a person has responded, their work is finished. They can now move on to other persons. It is inconceivable that in a great urban environment a person can be brought out of anonymity and obscurity, witnessed to, even led to a decision, and then allowed to slip back into that obscurity with no follow-up and discipling.

It is also true that some would place such a high emphasis on discipleship or "shepherding" that a Christian group can become ingrown, enjoying its own fellowship, and Bible study but doing little to reach out to others. It may be that in the urban setting this is the greater danger. The hunger for socialization, fellowship, and trusting relationships can be so great that when a group is formed, it can rapidly isolate itself.

The urban missionary should be allowed to develop skills in that witnessing methodology which best fits his or her personality and which are the most effective. Various methods of discipleship should be taught and tried in order to discover which one will work best. Missionaries need to be acquainted with a number of good methods which have worked for others. They need to be familiar with available materials to support these methods. Historically, Bible school and seminary training have given attention to this. It would seem rather urgent that added to this cognitive teaching would be an extensive practical experience in the urban setting under good supervision.

Witnessing as a life-style. The urban evangelist needs to be able to establish a life-style of evangelism. A great deal of evangelism today is event oriented. That is, evangelism events are periodically scheduled and all energies are directed toward a successful conducting of the events. Too often less time is given to following up on the results of the events. Such event-oriented evangelism is needed from time to time in urban areas and missionaries should be trained in these techniques. It may be that the greatest result of such evangelism is the stimulation of widespread interest in the non-Christian and nominal Christian population and in the pulling together by the Christian community in a common cause.

However, the evangelist who would plant his life in a vast urban community will have to be more involved on a daily basis than event-oriented evangelism allows. Unless there is a conscious daily effort made to broaden his circle of contacts and influence, he can soon find himself isolated and slipping into the same anonymity and depersonalized existence as many of those who live around him. Training for urban evangelism ought to include as a permeating force the discipline of a life-style of witnessing. It is an established fact that when relationships are formed, witness given, and continued follow-up provided, a more stable response to the gospel will occur.

Mission Action

Understanding cultures. The urban evangelist should be able to relate meaningfully to the cultures and people in the urban environment. It is absolutely necessary to be aware of the tremendous influence and impact of various cultures present in any urban area.

Several years ago I was involved in a major training conference for urban evangelists in Asia. The participants went out in teams into various sections of the city of Manila, the Philippines, to give practical application to what was being taught. In two hours my team had located and mapped the boundaries of three distinct and separate Filipino cultures and language groups in one small section of the city. Had an effort been made to establish a witness in each of these cultural communities, it would have been good to study carefully these cultures, understand the people, and bring the gospel witness in terms appropriate to their environment and cultural characteristics. Whether a foreign urban evangelist or a local national evangelist should begin the work, it is necessary to choose someone who will learn and appreciate that particular people with their unique culture.

Some years ago I· was involved in an analysis of a struggling Chinese congregation in the city of Saigon, Vietnam. It was discovered that one of the primary reasons for its lack of growth was that the leader of the group spoke Cantonese. The church itself was located in an area primarily populated by Fukien-speaking Chinese. Most of the small congregation spoke Swatow. Even though all of the Christians were able to communicate adequately in these languages, there were unique and powerful cultural differences which inhibited the outreach of the congregation. Certainly the pastor was at a disadvantage since his own cultural and language background differed from those with whom he worked.

The urban evangelist in America learns quickly that even in America where English is the dominant language, the various cultural influences indigenous to particular areas of America are extremely powerful and at times inhibiting. Unless urban evangelists learn to bridge these cultural gaps through understanding and appreciation, they will not be very effective with Christian witness.

One who anticipates working in the urban context would do well to be trained in a technique called "ethnographic interviewing" pioneered by the late James S. Spradley. Ethnographic interviewing is a technique by which one seeks to learn significant cultural information from a person who bears that culture. It is a methodological approach to the understanding and appreciation of an individual of another culture so that communication can occur. Whenever two people of different cultural backgrounds meet, there will always be feelings of separation. These feelings begin to fade, however, when effective communication occurs. The object, of course, is neither to surrender one's own culture nor to seek the surrender of the other's culture; it is to bridge the gap between the two. James Spradley has written several important books on this subject: *The Ethnographic Interview* published in 1979; *The Cultural Experience,* 1972; *The Cultural Prospective,* 1975. These give good insight into this exciting method. Training for work in urban evangelism should include not only a good understanding of ethnographic interviewing but should provide an actual working experience with it.

Assessing human needs. The urban evangelist should be able to assess human need and to respond intelligently and constructively. When one lives in the press of humankind, there is a constant awareness of human need in all its varying degrees. Missionaries often walk a fine line between two extremes. On the one hand, they may see so much need all about them that they are overwhelmed by it and begin to identify strongly with those who are in need. If they are not careful their perspective is affected. They begin to have as much need as the needy. On the other hand, they may see so much need that they feel unable to help with much of it and in reaction begin to harden their hearts. The missionary no longer feels deeply the need and thus loses the ability to minister. It is a sad time when one can walk daily in the midst of human need and not be able to see and feel that need. It is equally distressing when one walks in the midst of human need, feels it so deeply, and is then crippled by the emotions that are stirred by human needs.

Urban evangelists will walk that fine line between these two extremes occasionally drifting to one side or the other. They must have some way of checking their perspectives and an ability to recover a balance. Again, the ability to assess need and motivate people is key. Any training program for someone working in the urban setting ought to deal in depth with good principles of Christian social ministries. Whether missionaries are engaging most of their time in Christian social ministries or in evangelism, they need a good understanding of basic principles of Christian social ministries.

For many years evangelical Christianity steered away from social involvement lest it be seen as a "social gospel." In more recent years there have been attempts to note the relevance of the gospel to the social setting. Especially in urban areas the church must be seen as relevant, touching life, and speaking to human need. In doing so, one of the most difficult tensions to resolve is on the one hand ministering to people simply because they need ministering to and on the other hand projecting human needs ministries as an evangelistic tool. The one is seen as "social gospel;" the other is seen as manipulating people toward a desired goal. Surely there are ways to minister to people in need in a manner which reconciles these two extremes and results in a deeper appreciation of the gospel in a sincere ministry to people.

A training program for the urban evangelist ought to include developing the ability to analyze broad social structures and their impact on life and witness. To minister to the "whole person," there should be some understanding of the social currents which surround persons in the urban setting and which create the pressures under which people must live.

Creative church planting. Evangelism that results in churches is the goal of all our foreign and domestic mission efforts. Yet the goal of reaching people and starting churches is often impeded by improper concepts of the New Testament church. So much of our view of what a church should be results from observing cultural forms of the church as developed to fit affluent, North American Protestantism. Missionaries should learn that it is often neither possible nor feasible, and certainly not warranted, to seek to establish an urban church which approximates one's own cultural and traditional requirements. When the clear and unmistakable essential principles of the New Testament church are used as a foundation, they have a way of transcending cultural and historical bias.

This problem is experienced most dramatically in the acquistion of buildings or facilities in which to house a church. In today's world it is financially impossible to purchase land in most urban centers and build a church building with traditional spire or steeple, furnish it with well-aportioned pews, and provide space for graded Sunday School classes, choirs, and all that is normally associated with "church." Unless there is a clear understanding of what a true church is as a body of believers, there will be frustration and dissatisfaction which comes through a sense of incompleteness.

The executive director of a national Baptist convention reflected his own frustration in an address to the Baptist mission in his country. He said that if starting new churches depends on acquiring land and building buildings, the convention would be able financially to start seven new churches in urban areas by the year 2000. Of course his appeal was for church planters to break away from traditional concepts and to launch into new and creative ways of planting New Testament churches. To do this one has to forego the trappings of traditional and cultural patterns and emphasize the true nature and characteristics of the church as the people of God.

Developing indigenous leadership. The urban evangelist must be able to develop indigenous church leadership. It is not enough to know how to study culture. It is not enough to learn New Testament ecclesiology. There must also be the ability to work with new Christians, to facilitate their development as effective leaders, and to see the church become truly natural in its environment. Too often, even after years of development, the success or failure of a church depends totally on the leadership of missionaries. There is no question that such leadership is important in the beginning of mission work in a new area, but the role of the missionary should change from a pastor to a trainer of indigenous pastors as quickly as possible. Nationals can reach nationals much more easily than can the foreign missionary.

The best of all possible approaches would be for the urban evangelist to be able to start new work, to develop leadership, and to move on confidently to begin other new works with each one becoming self-sufficient. Just as a flower flourishes naturally in its own appropriate environment, so a church must take on its own natural environmental characteristics. Until the church's leadership is indigenous, the church will never be able to become indigenous.

The urban evangelist, missionary, and pastor must be trained in developing leadership and must be convinced before starting ministry on the field that the indigenous approach is the best approach. Most of us want to do it all ourselves, but this kind of paternalism will only stifle and slow our efforts to begin a "Christian people movement" among an unreached population.

Philosophical Presuppositions Underlying Training Methodology

The way a person seeks information is shaped early in life. Most of our educational systems are basically "teaching" systems. That is, the system begins with a teacher who embodies a certain amount and kind of information. The teacher then attempts to impart that information to students who attempt to assimilate it for possible use. It is basically information-oriented material. The student may use it or forget it. Often there is little opportunity for feedback or assessment of how the student utilizes what he or she has received. Usually, a curriculum is established and an array of teachers brought in to teach the students until the process is completed, graduation occurs, and the students move out to apply whatever they can remember of what they have been taught.

The tragedy is that when students become workers they no longer have the teachers available to provide what they need to know. They must now adjust to a different kind of learning, a learning which occurs on the job. Unless that adjustment is made the result can be a long period of floundering and frustration. It may be that one of the worker's first challenges is to learn how to learn.

An alternative system of education begins with the learner and plunges him or her into situations which stimulate a need to learn and a desire to learn. Such an experience is designed to help students know the questions to ask. The educational process begins with where the learners are and attempts to lead them to the place they need to be. There is little doubt that experiential learning has a way of clarifying issues, opening new vistas, and stimulating the desire for more. Such learning increases the independence of the learner so that he or she is not inclined to wait to be taught. The student is motivated to find resources and to utilize them. Such training looks for many ways in which to involve the student actively in the learning process.

For example, the use of case studies brings an individual face-to-face with actual situations and the experience of finding solutions. Dialogue with persons who have walked that way before allows for vicarious experiences. Placing students in the appropriate milieu of life and helping them respond to that experience is an excellent way of learning. When these methodologies are applied, the result is a personal involvement in the process of learning.

Training for urban evangelization requires far more than the presentation of cognitive information in a teaching environment. It may begin there, but inevitably it will have to lead the student out into the streets of the city where people live, work, and experience life. The philosophy of education which undergirds training for urban evangelization will need to be experiential in nature. The use of case studies from various urban situations greatly enhances the learning process. Placing urban evangelists in direct dialogue will motivate and stimulate learning. Taking the evangelists into the city for studies in demography, sociology, culture, methods of witness, and discipling can never be substituted by lectures, books, articles, and the like. If urban evangelists can discipline themselves to learn how to learn from situations, people, and experiences, their effectiveness will dramatically increase.

The best way to come to grips with identity and self-concept is to place oneself in the midst of people. One really has to be in contact and in communication with urban people to understand who they are. A training program ought to have ways of placing a trainee under stress so that appropriate action can be taken to deal with stress. Experiencing stress and learning through it has a way of molding attitudes and forming character. An athlete cannot know how high he or she can jump until a bar is put in place and an attempt is made to leap over it. In the same manner, prospective urban evangelists cannot know really who they are as evangelists and how they relate to others and why they relate in that way until they actually walk the streets, feel the pressure, minister to people, and are blessed by good feedback from teachers who care.

It is difficult to understand feelings of alienation until you stand with a desire to relate to strangers and are shunned. You can study principles of dealing with alienation. You can be lectured on alienation. You can understand the nature of alienation. However, it takes experiencing the feelings of alienation to discover how to overcome such feelings. We never learn how to create and to make progress until we are faced with the need to create. We really never learn how to depend on others until we find ourselves helpless in the face of real difficulties beyond our control. Training can never be effective until it includes life-shaping experience.

A Final Note: Training and the Power of God

As we have seen, the masses of people in the cities of the world and the acute physical, social, emotional, and spiritual needs create a tension to do something. We want to respond and to do so effectively. In this concern we naturally see the need for training in order that what we do in the name of Christ will do the most good. This is only good stewardship, yet it is easy to forget that we cannot succeed through our own strength. The Lord has a way of reminding us of this from time to time.

The story is told of a short-order cook in a small restaurant in southern California who became a radiant Christian. Within a few weeks of that experience he learned that a team of laypersons was going to Mexico to repair a small church building which had been destroyed by a storm. This man went to the team saying that he knew nothing about construction work but would like very much to go along with the team if he could be of help. Enthusiastically, they invited him to go along as their cook. Upon arrival at their destination the team was graciously received by the congregation. As an expression of their love and gratitude, the congregation introduced one of the finest cooks in town to cook for the team during their stay.

The layman cook was deeply distressed. His initial feeling was that his one reason for being there had now been taken away. Seeing the construction team working skillfully at their craft and feeling his own inadequacy, he walked rather dejectedly away from the construction site. Soon he stopped to watch a lone Mexican carpenter who was engaged in building a small house. He noticed that the carpenter had to climb down from the roof, retrieve a few boards, and carry them back up to the roof to nail them. Recognizing the slowness of this method and evident fatigue in the carpenter, the cook began to hand the boards up to the carpenter as he needed them.

The carpenter became distressed and began to speak loudly and rapidly in Spanish which the cook could not understand. Someone stopped by upon hearing the commotion and interpreted for the two men. It seems the carpenter had no money to pay for the assistance of the cook and was anxious about what would be demanded. The cook, upon understanding the problem, was able to communicate that he wanted nothing from the carpenter except a chance to help and to do something meaningful.

All day the two men toiled, enjoying their newfound friendship which had now overcome their inability to communicate. When evening arrived, the cook accepted his friend's invitation to go home with him for dinner. As they sat in the humble dwelling of the carpenter they were pressed in on every side by the sounds and physical presence of many neighbors. The two men worked at communicating with each other. The carpenter's son served as an interpreter as best he could.

The cook began to share how he had met Jesus a few weeks before coming to Mexico. He shared what had happened to him since that time. He told of the joy and peace which was now dramatically controlling his life. He explained that it was because of Jesus Christ that he had come to Mexico. He read a few verses from the Bible which were significant in his own life. The carpenter was fascinated by the simple testimony about Jesus. He was so overcome by the story that he invited the cook to return the next night so that some of his neighbors could hear the story.

The cook knew his shortcomings as a preacher, Bible teacher, and missionary. He explained to the people that he was very new in his faith in Jesus Christ and could tell them little beyond what he himself had experienced. The interest was so great that many of them decided that they too wanted to become Christians. The cook then called for a local Baptist missionary to come and help him. Today a strong church stands in that great urban neighborhood where a humble layman once stood and told as simply as he knew how what Jesus meant in his life.

The story reveals a man who overcame his identity crisis. His loneliness and dejection became forces which drove him to find meaning and expression. His feeling of incompetence led him back to basic things which he could do and which in turn led him to the cutting edges of his limits of competency. His success was not the result of a great deal of training. What he was able to accomplish came from who he was in Jesus Christ. What he did grew out of his personal knowledge and experience with Jesus and through the power of the Holy Spirit.

It is not a desire in this chapter to deify certain kinds of training experience. It is common knowledge that many people have been effective as evangelists in the urban setting without a great deal of formal training. However, it is also clear that effectiveness can be greatly enhanced by good training. The cook was able to overcome his adversity, his sense of incompetence, and his lack of a sense of meaning by placing himself in a situation where he had to come to grips with himself. Though the experience did not begin as a training exercise for this man, it fulfilled all of these requirements.

Hopefully, the education and training of future urban evangelists will consist of life-shaping experiences which will result in urban evangelists who are fulfilled and effective.

10

Commitment to the Future

William R. O'Brien

The last half of the twentieth century has birthed new meaning for the two prefixes *micr-* and *macr-*. The microscopic world has become visible through modern technology and the macrocosmic also has been brought into our visibility. We are now trying to understand what we see at either end of reality. These particular dimensions of life are priorities for a relative few: scientists, philosophers, educators, some theologians, and others, but there is one reality that affects all persons—indeed it is a product of humankind, namely more and more humankind!

With six billion persons on earth by 2000, one would think the whole planet would appear as a single macropolis. If we were looking at planet earth from the moon, however, it would appear quite differently. What one would see would be a clustering of humankind in compacted land areas. One city after another would resemble dense nuclei with free-floating rural protoplasm pulsating around these concentrations of humanity.

Alas, we who are earthbound do not have the luxury of a moon perspective. What would seem like a micropolis at that safe distance is really a macropolis or a megacity. The reader has already been exposed to staggering portraits of causes and consequences of the urban phenomenon. This layering of Homo sapiens in congested areas has been described by some as the focuses of loneliness, alienation, crime, immorality, and meaninglessness. But such concentrations of mind and personality also produce art, literature, music, museums, sports, and other endeavors that magnify the image of God in us.

So rather than bemoaning what is happening, as comanagers with the Lord of creation, let us seek to understand what is the mission of this purposive God. Is there some reason why such a large percentage of earth people will have moved to the city by AD 2000? Is the hand of God behind the reemergence of the city-state? Is the Holy Spirit patiently waiting for open minds to guide us into new ways of understanding our past and perceiving the future? Are new, exciting opportunities for networking and interdependence surfacing that can greatly accelerate the spread of the gospel? I both hope and presuppose that God is already in the city waiting for us!

We are at a unique crossroads. The Communications Era Task Force has published a document entitled *At the Crossroads.* In it they say, "We journey between the lightning and the thunder. We journey between the flash of recognition of what is happening to us and the reverberations of what we are willing to do about it." In that journey we must embrace new concepts, rise to new commitments, and exude new confidence.

New Concepts

Review

The only difference in the Garden of Eden and Paradise is one of population. It is not one of lordship or relationship. The problem of being outside the garden and outside Paradise, or the heavenly city, is one of both lordship and relationship. Human history is being played out between Genesis 1 and Revelation 22. It has been a cycle of clustering, disseminating, and reclustering. The drives for conquest and survival intertwined with the eras of agriculture and industry have affected how and where peoples have come together. Because the "outside-the-garden" nature of alienation has been so total, wherever people cluster the sin disease has affected every system and structure.

Gratefully, the Architect of shalom has never abandoned his purpose of combining the singular obedience of the "garden" with a congregated expression of it. Indeed, the very basis of shalom implies wholeness and cohesiveness of the multiple parts. So Abram, along with his descendants of faith, represents that thread of holy history that moves toward the holy city. Ultimately, the creative and covenantal Word of the Architect combines with a redemptive Calvary Word making fully possible the ultimate city.

The *ekklesia* of the New Testament understood themselves to be a "people" from among the people. They also understood in a unique and daring way they were not to withdraw from the world of people. Paul was a strategic thinker and implementer. The major cities of the Near East became the centers of proclaiming and redeeming activity. Paul knew the potential for impact resided in centers of power. He also knew the communications network enabled accelerated activity in population clusters. He was well aware rural life is influenced by the city—not the other way around.

The fall of Rome introduced an era of the "monastepolis." Christian witness was preserved in the monastery while feudalism replaced the role of the cities. It is interesting that the Dark Ages and the Enlightenment became the labels for eras that contrasted the dissemination of people groups with that of regathering.

With the reemergence of the city, there came the mix again of the "earthbound" with the "heavenly pilgrims." Some pilgrims chose to withdraw from the world. Some attempted to force the heavenly city on earth. Neither approach made enough impact to change increasingly complex patterns of non-relationship mirrored in crime, immorality, pollution, poverty, and alienation. The city became secularized, and too often the church's way of coping with it was to insulate itself, enabling it to gather in a holy huddle and praise Jesus, singing about the heavenly city while ignoring the one in which they lived. Meanwhile, the mandate has not changed. To hallow him who is in the heavenly city is to pray and work that his will might be done in the cities on earth.

Throughout this book the urban phenomenon of the late twentieth century has been reinforced. There will be at least 500 world-class cities by the end of the century. No "Tuesday night visitation program" can affect such clusters. Indeed, even the hint of that and other related rural and village models imply a lack of understanding of what is happening—a total unwillingness to stand between the lightning and the thunder. There must be intensive study of what is happening, followed by a willingness to incarnate the gospel in city terms. Not even "rurbanity" is sufficient, that is, a rural mind-set living in the city.

Projection

What is happening? We may well be experiencing the rebirth of city-states. To be sure they would be more regional than the old city-states, but there is identifiable core and circumference. Even as people may choose to live out beyond the crunch of population, their lives will still revolve around what happens in the city.

In the technological Northern Hemisphere these city-states will have a regional-type governing coordination. They already have their own museums, concert halls, symphonies, ballets, operas, regional magazines, sports coliseums, community college systems, health maintenance organizations, and gerontology centers. Increasingly, they will have diversified noncoercive educational centers, both academic and vocational. They have both corporate and branch offices of global or multinational corporations. They all have up-link and down-link capacities in the instantaneous global communications network.

In the Southern Hemisphere, cities tend to be configured differently and for various reasons, but the end result is the same in terms of concentration of people, problems, and potential except that it is often more dense and complex. In both hemispheres, world-class cities may be characterized by function as Raymond Bakke has pointed out. Some are administrative, others smokestack, while yet others are cultural in makeup. It is this combination of city-state, multinational business, and global communications network that is modifying the role of federal governments, causing them to be brokers in negotiating processes rather than insulated national entities making unilaterial decisions in their own self-interests.

People of God within these larger human concentrations must minister on two fronts simultaneously. We must compassionately relate to the victims of this transition, the harrassed and the helpless. At the same time, we must passionately push on the structures and systems that by chance or choice continue to victimize. Further, we must daily be proclaiming salvation and hope to previctims who are simply trying to cope. The mission of our God is certainly larger than the "hope to cope," but it does include that.

New Commitment

Christians must venture away from their havens whether they be provincial or churchly, but the venture must be one of will and foresight. God forbid that we would timidly back into this opportunity. As Jaoa Falcoa of Brazil has said, "The problem of reaching the city does not lie within the city. It lies within the church." A change of mind calls for a new commitment.

We are rapidly moving to a world of cities full of a "world of people." That statement is both quantitative and descriptive. Not only are cities populous, but they are multiracial and multilingual. We are living in an era of global diaspora. Majorities are not nearly as major and minorities are not nearly as minor as they once were. The mixture is further characterized by extremes of poshness and poverty. Palatial houses, high-rise condos, modern suburbia, squatter villages, residential slums, streets, and doorways are the addresses of city dwellers.

A plurality of world views and religious expressions are held in all strata. There has been no containment policy of any of the living religions or any of the emerging cults and new religions. Islam, Hinduism, Krishna Consciousness, and the Unification Church, for example, are all present in the Bible belt of the United States. We are not even faring well at how to guarantee their freedoms much less at how to meaningfully proclaim and live out the Christian faith among them. We must bring a new commitment to learning how to be Christian while witnessing to our faith with non-Christians.

The new commitment will move us from a partial to a holistic biblical posture. William McIlvaney has warned us about accepting Scriptures that comfort our afflictions while ignoring the ones that afflict our comforts. W. O. Carver used to ask his missions classes at The Southern Baptist Theological Seminary, "What's the Bible all about? Is it *all* about anything?" It is all about one thing: the creative and redemptive purpose of God for all people. Understanding our comanagerial responsibility in this cosmic mission should force us to take seriously the whole counsel of God. We must not manipulate Scripture by declaring it divine, then practicing selective application.

The new commitment must move us from a provincial to a global posture. In doing that we do not lose sight of the local. To the contrary, we will view it more healthily. The local/global focus is the only perspective befitting a Christian. It forces one not only to be aware of what is happening globally but to become learners through that awareness. The models in this book from Nairobi, Bangkok, and Singapore are not just missionary stories. They are living models that are worthy of study. That study should be in depth, reflecting context and variables. Often a creative and charismatic leader is the catalyst for impacting all the variables within the context. It is rarely successful when one tries to emulate or reproduce the successful model without identifying the effect of the leadership chemistry in the situation. Nevertheless, we must be seeking transferables and the potential for cross-fertilization.

The new commitment will elevate us above the national to a Kingdom mind-set. While Christ will allow himself to be communicated through any culture, he will not be trapped in it. We should be genuinely appreciative of the finest dimensions of our heritage. But Kingdom citizens are pilgrims. Pilgrims do not idolize their culture—they are passing through. As the world has become increasingly complex and pluralistic, we are often tempted to go for the fast fix. Unwilling to become suffering servants in the cities (or anywhere else), we too easily opt for the Constantinian formula marrying the religious to the civil. The challenge for any believer is one that keeps us in constant tension. We stand within the system in order to bring life from death. At the same time we are called to stand over against our culture with a prophetic voice. And we weep with him who said, "O Jerusalem, Jerusalem" (Luke 13:34).

The new commitment will bring a conscious, willful choice to be in the city, learn the city, train to be effective in the city. No pious talk will do. Involvement is the price of commitment.

New Confidence

The soldiers took Jesus outside the city and crucified him. On the first day of the week Mary of Magdala made the discovery of the empty tomb. Later that morning she became the bearer of good news to the other disciples. That evening Jesus appeared among them with greetings of shalom and the commission, "As the Father has sent me, I am sending you" (John 20:21, NIV). What could so few do in cities like Jerusalem, Ephesus, Athens, Corinth, and Rome? No cars, planes, printing press, radio, television, telephone, or satellites!

Within sixty years John wrote again, this time about a vision. For him it matched the reality of what had already begun to happen with the reality of how it would all end.

Revelation 7:9-10 (NIV)

> After this I looked and there before me was a great multitude that no one could count, from every nation, tribe, people and language, standing before the throne and in front of the Lamb. They were wearing white robes and were holding palm branches in their hands. And they cried out in a loud voice: "Salvation belongs to our God,/ who sits on the throne,/and to the Lamb."

Revelation 21:1-3 (NIV)

> Then I saw a new heaven and a new earth, for the first heaven and the first earth had passed away, and there was no longer any sea. I saw the Holy City, the new Jerusalem, coming down out of heaven from God, prepared as a bride beautifully dressed for her husband. And I heard a loud voice from the throne saying, "Now the dwelling of God is with men, and he will live with them. They will be his people, and God himself will be with them and be their God."

The bridge between now and then is a unique word.

Matthew 28:16-20 (NIV)

> Then the eleven disciples went to Galilee, to the mountain where Jesus had told them to go. When they saw him, they worshiped him; but some doubted. Then Jesus came to them and said, "All authority in heaven and on earth has been given to me. Therefore go and make

disciples of all nations, baptizing them in the name of the Father and of the Son and of the Holy Spirit, and teaching them to obey everything I have commanded you. And surely I will be with you always, to the very end of the age."

All authority is his. He makes both it and his presence available to us. How comforting! But firmly fixed between the declarations of power and presence is a *command*. And it follows that the power-presence is only available to those who are in the middle of *obeying* the command! The fact that he has all power and the fact of his promise to go with us are truths not to be denied. But in this context, taken alone they are half-truths, and a half-truth is heresy.

Christians must not surrender the cities in hopelessness. That is fatalism. We must not retreat from the cities. That is defeatism. We must not hide in the cities. That is cowardice. Like the salt and light we are, we will infiltrate and penetrate the cities as humble change agents. Foward—serve!

Contributors

Raymond J. Bakke is professor of ministry at Northern Baptist Theological Seminary in Lombard, Illinois.

Winston Crawley is vice president for planning, Foreign Mission Board of the Southern Baptist Convention, Richmond, Virginia.

Francis M. DuBose is professor of missions, Golden Gate Baptist Theological Seminary, Mill Valley, California.

David Finnell is church growth research consultant, evangelism department of the Singapore Baptist Convention, Singapore.

C. Kirk Hadaway is research director, Center for Urban Church Studies, Nashville, Tennessee.

Ervin E. Hastey is senior consultant for evangelism and church growth ministries, Foreign Mission Board.

Ronald Hill is a missionary assigned to Bangkok, Thailand, Foreign Mission Board.

Samuel M. James is director, orientation and furlough department, Foreign Mission Board.

Jimmy Maroney is associate to the area director for east and southern Africa, Foreign Mission Board.

William R. O'Brien is executive vice president, Foreign Mission Board.

R. Keith Parks is president, Foreign Mission Board.

Larry L. Rose is executive director, Center for Urban Church Studies.

A. Clark Scanlon is executive assistant to the senior vice president, office of overseas operations, Foreign Mission Board.

M. Thomas Starkes is Chester L. Quarles professor of Christian missions and world religion, New Orleans Baptist Theological Seminary, New Orleans, Louisiana.